Terry Copp, Matt Symes, Caitlin
McWilliams, Nick Lachance,
Geoff Keelan & Jeffrey W. Mott

1812

A Guide to the War and its Legacy

LCMSDS Press of Wilfrid Laurier University

© LCMSDS Press of Wilfrid Laurier Univeristy, Waterloo, Ontario. 2013

0 1 2 3 4 5 6 7 8 9

Printed in Canada

Library and Archives Canada Cataloguing in Publication

1812 : a guide to the war and its legacy / Terry Copp ... [et al.].

Includes bibliographical references.
ISBN 978-1-926804-13-2

1. Canada--History--War of 1812. 2. United States--History--
War of 1812. 3. Canada--History--War of 1812--Battlefields--
Guidebooks. I. Copp, Terry, 1938- II. Title: Eighteen twelve.

FC442.E43 2013   971.03'4   C2013-900706-7

Cover Design: Matt Symes
Text design and formatting: Matt Symes
Cover Photo: The Brock Monument. [Matt Symes]
History Section: War of 1812 battle scene with soldiers
and Indians [Felix Darley cica 1860, LC-2010715547]
Tour Section: Where General Brock fell.
[Toronto Public Library JRR 1299 CAB IV]
Additional Information: A soldier's kit.
[Caitlin McWilliams]

FSC
www.fsc.org
MIX
Paper from
responsible sources
FSC® C016245

Contents

List of Maps

Preface

The Laurier Centre for Military Strategic and Disarmament Studies at Wilfrid Laurier University published its first battlefield guidebook, *A Canadian's Guide to the Battle of Normandy*, in 1994 and we now have six titles for the Canadian experience in the Second World War, as well as our recently published *Canadian Battlefields 1915 – 1918*, in print. *1812: The War and its Legacy*, is modelled on our First World War guidebook. The history section, intended to provide context and a brief description of the key battles, has been written by Terry Copp. Jeffrey W. Mott added the historical context of the war in what is now New Brunswick and Nova Scotia. The information on places to visit is the work of Caitlin McWilliams, Geoff Keelan, Nick Lachance, Matt Symes, Terry Copp, and Jeffrey W. Mott. The maps were designed by Nick Lachance and we owe a special thanks to Google Earth for allowing us to reproduce the satellite imagery in our guides. Nick Lachance Caitlin McWilliams, Linda Risacher Copp and Matt Symes took most of the modern day photographs in the text. The historical imagery has largely been acquired from the rich archives of the Library of Congress, Library and Archives Canada, the Department of National Defence, Parks Canada, and the National Parks Services in the United States. Matt Symes was responsible for the design of the book.

Beyond those names that appear on the front cover, the Centre has a number of students and friends who are committed and passionate about the work at LCMSDS. The Centre gives meaningful opportunities to a select group of high achieving students and some deserve special mention for their work on this project. Johanna Boeringa, a 2nd year student at WLU, has poured countless hours into editing the guide for consistency, tracking down GPS coordinates, and even contributed a few sentences as well as a photo to the final product. *1812: A Guide to the War and Its Legacy* is a stronger product on account of her initiative and enthusiasm. Kellen Kurschinski has a keen eye for detail and his edits have made this guide a stronger product. Brandey (Barton) Smythe, a former graduate student at WLU, gave generously of her time on various versions of this text. This small paragraph hardly seems to do justice to the countless hours those associated with the centre spent searching images, chasing down articles, proofing for consistency and doing what we do best in here – finding a way to get the job done.

The Milton F. Gregg Centre for the Study of War and Society at the University of New Brunswick (unb.ca/greggcentre) has emerged as our closest partner in the quest to foster education, research and discussion of historical and contemporary conflict. Their book series focused on New Brunswick's military past has produced more than 16 volumes, three of which focus on the War of 1812. Marc Milner, the Director of the Gregg

Centre, put us in touch with Jeffrey W. Mott and offered feedback on the Maritime sections of the text. That this book incorporates the history of the war on the East Coast and two excellent tours in the picturesque provinces of New Brunswick and Nova Scotia is the result of our strong partnership. J. Brent Wilson, who works for the Gregg Centre and closely with the museums in New Brunswick, looked over the text and his last-minute edits helped immensely.

The 200th anniversary of the War of 1812 prompted the Government of Canada to encourage or develop a wide variety of commemorative activities, including new interpretation centres at important sites. Television commercials offering a simplified, patriotic message have added to publicity about the bicentennial celebrations. Critics of the current government have argued that focusing attention on the war is part of a larger project to replace the image of Canada as a nation committed to peacekeeping with ideas about Canada as a "warrior nation." As on-site research for this book was made possible through a grant from the Department of National Defence through its Security and Defence Forum, it is important to note that, as has been the case throughout the history of that program, there has been no attempt to influence our approach to the subject. We believe the War of 1812 was an important event in North American history with lasting consequences for Canadians, Americans, and the First Nations. Our objective in the historical section is to increase understanding of what happened and why it happened that way. In the tour section we take you to the key locations and offer an explanation of the fluid memory that has evolved over the last 200 years.

Since the Centre's operational funding from the Security and Defence forum was cut by the Department of National Defence early 2012, we have been forced to seek unique ways to raise enough money to keep the operations of LCMSDS afloat. Our board of directors has worked with Terry Copp to ensure we will survive for the immediate future. To fund a portion of this book, we launched a campaign through canadianmilitaryhistory.ca. Several people pre-ordered the book to show their support. Some dug deeper and gave generously and their commitment to this publication deserves special mention. Cliff Mess joined us on a tour of the 1812 sites in Niagara and his contribution toward the design is greatly appreciated. Jeffrey Austin, Karen Almadi, William Fenrick, the Fitzgerald-Black family, and Rych Mills also found a way to support our guide. Thank you!

Finally, we wish to thank John and Pattie Cleghorn for their continuing support of LCMSDS and this project.

Anglo-American Conflict

To understand the conflict that led to the War of 1812 we must begin with the Treaty of 1783 that ended the War of Independence. The treaty was deliberately generous to the Americans. Recognizing their independence was a military necessity but other clauses, especially the transfer of the territory between the Appalachians and the Ohio River to the United States, ignored the interests of both the First Nations who had fought for the British and the Québec-based fur traders.

The British Prime Minister, Lord Shelburne, a disciple of Adam Smith and a friend of the utilitarian philosopher Jeremy Bentham, was convinced that the British Empire would best be served by free trade and harmonious relations with the United States. A peace treaty that gave Americans everything they could wish for would, Shelburne believed, guarantee good relations and prosperity for Britain within an informal empire.

This strategy was challenged by Shelburne's opponents, particularly British shipping interests, and the government fell. His successor, William Pitt the Younger, generally agreed with Shelburne but had to compromise. The Navigation Acts excluding American ships from trade within the Empire were enforced and British troops continued to occupy forts in the Ohio Valley, encouraging First Nations to oppose American expansion into the region.

When revolutionary France declared war on Britain in 1793 there was a new incentive to avoid conflict with America and so the British signed the Treaty of London of 1794 promising to evacuate the Ohio Valley and arbitrate other differences. Known commonly as Jay's Treaty after the American Chief

Lord Shelburne. [Jean-Laurent Mosnier]

William Pitt the Younger. [John Hoppner]

History

11

Justice of the Supreme Court and treaty negotiator John Jay, it was widely opposed in America as it failed to deal with the British trade restrictions, the impressment of seamen from American ships, and the seizure of American vessels caught trading with France. Thomas Jefferson and James Madison were the leading critics of the treaty and they began to shape a political party, the Republicans, in opposition to the dominant Federalists.

Meanwhile, American military power was brought to bear on the First Nations. General Anthony Wayne and his troops overwhelmed Shawnee and Delaware warriors at the Battle of Fallen Timbers (1795). First Nations leaders were forced to accept the Treaty of Greenville which ceded most of Ohio and gave the United States additional blocks of territory beyond the "Greenville Line." By 1796, British troops had withdrawn to St. Joseph's Island, Amherstburg, and Fort George, but British "Indian Agents" maintained relationships with First Nations living south of the border.

The unresolved differences between the British Empire and the United States of America escalated after the resumption of war between Britain and France in 1803. Nelson's destruction of the French and Spanish fleets at the Battle of Trafalgar in 1805 removed any challenge to Britain's control of the seas and the Royal Navy was told to prevent foreign - especially American - shipping from supplying Britain's enemies. The United States responded to this with a series of restrictive trade measures intended to force Britain to recognize the rights of neutrals. This strategy failed to have any impact on the British government which was totally focused on the life and death struggle with Napoleon Bonaparte.

James Madison, President of the United States. [Thomas Sully, LC-USZ62-75384]

Thomas Jefferson, President of the United States. [R. Peale, LC-USZ62-16960]

The Signing of the Treaty of Greene Ville. [Howard Chandler Christie, 1923]

The most serious single incident in this cold war occurred in 1807 when the HMS *Leopard* tricked the U.S. Navy's frigate *Chesapeake* into stopping and then demanded the surrender of alleged deserters. When the American captain refused, the *Leopard* fired several broadsides and killed three crew members. This unprovoked, illegal attack was certainly grounds for war, particularly since the British government failed to make immediate restitution but President Thomas Jefferson was determined to avoid a hot war, simply ordering British warships to leave American waters.

James Madison succeeded Jefferson as President in 1808. Madison continued Jefferson's policies but he lacked the popularity and loyal support that marked Jefferson's tenure. He was also faced with a revival of the Federalist Party which favoured cooperation with the British war effort.

The *Chesapeake-Leopard* Affair. [Fred S. Cozzens, 1897]

Continued British involvement in the American Northwest was a second source of tension. Madison, like Jefferson, genuinely believed that the First Nations in the Ohio and Mississippi valleys needed to accept the reality of American settlement, giving up their traditional way of life and their land. He insisted that the First Nations living beyond the Greenville Line were "always free to say 'no'" to selling their lands but the actions of the government, the settlers, and land speculators revealed the hypocrisy of his policy.

The Americans, who had obtained the vast Louisiana Territory by purchase from France in 1803, assumed that the lands between the Appalachians and the Mississippi River would soon be settled so they were determined to obtain the consent of the First Nations by purchase, or outright force. William Henry Harrison, who was appointed Governor of the sizable Indiana Territory in 1800, was the principal agent of American expansion. After the *Chesapeake* incident he was convinced that British intrigue was responsible for First Nations resistance to his plans for further land acquisition and his views were shared in Washington.

The Division of Ohio - "White and Indian lands determined at the Treaty of Greenville" originally published in William Peters, *Ohio Lands and their Subdivisions* (1918), p. 98.

First Nations Strategy

There were at least twelve identifiable First Nations groups living in the American Northwest in 1812. All were conscious of the tribe or nation they belonged to but their primary identification was with family or village and intermarriage was common. All of them except the Wyandot spoke a variant of the Algonquian language, employed women in agriculture, and maintained male gender roles as hunters or warriors. Hereditary chiefs lacked the power to control individuals who chose to raid other villages or white settlements. There was no central authority to speak for individual First Nations let alone a coalition among them.

Population estimates are notoriously difficult and are usually based on extrapolations from the number of warriors thought to be available. It seems likely that the total population of First Nations in the Ohio-Great Lakes region could not have been more than 50,000 in 1810. By then there were 7.5 million Americans, more than one million of whom had migrated west of the Appalachians with more arriving each day. The Ohio River and its tributaries were major roads for settlers and the residents of the Ohio and Indiana territories were confident statehood would follow settlement.

Spirit of The Frontier painted in 1872 by John Gast is a visual representation of Manifest Destiny – The religious belief that the United States should expand from the Atlantic to the Pacific in the name of God.

The Shawnee Prophet [seated] *and Tecumseh* [Standing to the right]. [LC-USZ62-19460]

The steady encroachment on lands beyond the Greenville Line reached a climax in 1809 when Governor Harrison coerced some First Nations chiefs into signing the Treaty of Fort Wayne which ceded additional land in Indiana to the Americans. The treaty fuelled First Nations resistance and provided Tenskwatawa, "the Shawnee Prophet," and his brother Tecumseh with broad support for their vision of a land freed from the "long knives" who the Prophet said "grew from the scum of the Great Water when it was troubled by evil spirits." Tecumseh shared this vision and sought to create a warriors' confederacy that would openly oppose further land transfers, by force if necessary.

Harrison understood the threat posed by the Prophet and Tecumseh and "had no doubt that the present hostile disposition of the Prophet and his Votaries has been produced by British interference." By December of 1810, Harrison was convinced that the concentration of warriors at Prophetstown, on the Tippecanoe River, threatened the Indiana-Ohio frontier requiring pre-emptive military action. On 24 June 1811 Harrison directly addressed Tecumseh, warning him that "the handful of men you have about you" are no match for the power in the "Seventeen Fires" (the seventeen American states and territories) or the "Kentucky Fire alone" which will pour forth "as numerous as the mosquitoes on the shores of the Wabash."

Tecumseh replied saying he would visit Harrison "to wash away all those bad stories" but the meeting, held at Vincennes in early August 1811, aggravated the situation. Tecumseh announced that he had united the Northern Tribes who were now under his direction and he would soon "visit the Southern Tribes to get them to unite with those of the north." Harrison informed the Secretary of War that Tecumseh's absence "affords a most favorable opportunity for breaking up his Confederacy" and on 20 September a force of regulars and militia began the advance from Vincennes to Prophetstown. The battle that followed, known as Tippecanoe, began when the Prophet led a night attack on the American encampment. Losses were about equal but when dawn broke the settlement on the Tippecanoe River had been abandoned, allowing Harrison to burn the houses and destroy crops. Harrison thus set the stage for an intensified frontier war which merged into the war declared in June 1812.

After the Battle of Tippecanoe, the First Nations of the Northwest had three strategic options: accept subordination to the United States, migrate to lands remote from American settlement, or attempt to revive the confederacy and join the British in a war to establish a separate "buffer state" in the northwest. Adapt, leave, or fight. The divisions that had long marked the First Nations

The Battle of Tippecanoe. [Kurtz and Allison, 1889]

made unified action impossible and all three strategies were pursued by various groups at various times.

Tecumseh and other lesser-known but important First Nations leaders, especially Stayeghtha (Roundhead), decided that their best hope lay in alliance with the British. A victory over the Americans was, they believed, the only basis for the establishment of a separate First Nations territory. On 13 March 1812, Tecumseh sent a delegation to Amherstburg to seal the alliance but Matthew Elliot, their Indian Agent, was still following orders to avoid any action that might provoke the Americans. The declaration of war in June ended British hesitation.

A sketch for the regents speech on Mad-ass-son's insanity. Gabriel blowing the message "A bad news for you" at James Madison, who is standing between Napoleon and the devil, as two women symbolizing Great Britain and America and British soldiers look on.
[George Cruikshank, LC-USZC4-5917]

Mr. Madison's War: A Strategy

Why did the President of the United States, who knew his country was deeply divided on the issue, seek congressional support for a declaration of war? The immediate cause was the growing conflict within Madison's own party orchestrated by a variety of "malcontents" unhappy with his leadership. The arrival in Washington of a new British Ambassador, Augustus Foster, offered a chance of avoiding war but when James Moore, the Secretary of State, learned that Foster's instructions were to settle the *Chesapeake* affair and not to restore the rights of neutrals or end impressment, Madison decided to call Congress into session in November 1811. He declared that "the time has arrived to put the United States into armour" by expanding the regular army, militia, and navy while increasing the supply of war material, especially weapons and ammunition for land warfare.

Speaker of the House, Henry Clay. [M. Jouett]

The message pleased the Speaker of the House, Henry Clay of Kentucky, and other young congressmen from the south and west known as "Warhawks" but it did nothing to persuade members to agree to the taxes necessary to finance a war. By 1 June 1812, when Madison asked Congress for a formal declaration of war, little had been done to prepare for an armed conflict. Opposition from the Federalist leaders in New England and anti-Madison Republicans had grown as the votes for war, 79-49 in the House and 19-13 in the Senate, illustrated.

Madison's war message listed familiar grievances: impressment, illegal blockades, the Orders-in-Council restricting neutral trade, and the responsibility of British Indian Agents for the renewal of warfare on the Western frontier. None of these issues were new or particularly acute, so why did the United States decide to try and invade and occupy Great Britain's North American colonies in 1812? The most persuasive answer is offered by University of Virginia historian J.C.A. Stagg who has worked closely with the Madison Papers. His book, *Mr. Madison's War*, is the most comprehensive study of the politics of the era available. Stagg writes:

with a total population of barely half a million, the various provinces of Canada seemed to be the weakest links in the chain of British imperial power and many Americans assumed that they could be easily seized by the United States with its vastly superior population of nearly seven and

History

one half million. Yet Canada did not seem in itself to be the source of the most important grievances that the United States wish to settle by war... For this reason, most opponents of the war never ceased to point out that the conquest of Canada promised neither to guarantee respect for American maritime rights nor even to reimburse the nation for the expense of the effort.

Stagg argues that for Madison "the policy of a Canadian war followed logically from his previous diplomatic strategies." American policy under both Jefferson and Madison had been based on the assumption that the British Empire needed raw materials from North America. Legislative efforts to restrict British access to these resources had failed partly because the Canadas and adjacent parts of the northern United States provided the wheat, timber, and other commodities the British required. Once Canada was conquered, Madison believed the British would have to make peace on American terms both at sea and on the Western Frontier.

Grand Master of the noble order of the Two Cod Fishes. Caricature of wealthy American politician and civic reformer Josiah Quincy, who was an opponent of the War of 1812. Quincy stands stiffly on a rocky shore while fish frolic in the sea behind him. He wears a crown and a regal red and gold coat on whose breast is a pair of crossed codfish. He holds a scepter in his left hand, and says, "I Josiah the first do by this my Royal Proclamation announce myself King of New England, Novia Scotia and Passamaquoddy. [LC-DIG-ppmsc-05876]

Madison's War: Operational Plans

Madison's belief that the conquest of Canada would force the British Empire to redress American grievances and respect American sovereignty was based more on hope than evidence. His ideas about military operations to achieve strategic objectives were equally uncertain. If Britain was to be dislodged from North America, the key objectives were Québec City and Halifax yet neither Madison nor his Secretary of War, William Eustis, had even the vaguest idea of how these citadels of British power might be taken. Given the strength of the British fleet, no seaborne attack on Nova Scotia was possible and New England's opposition to the war made an advance from Maine into New Brunswick highly problematic. To approach Québec the Americans first needed to capture Montréal and perhaps Kingston before advancing east to Québec. There they would have to deal with the British fleet as well as the city's formidable defences.

The Republican war enthusiasts ignored such obvious realities comforting themselves with simplistic and bombastic statements such as Clay's declaration that "the militia of Kentucky are alone competent to place Montréal and Upper Canada at our feet." When questioned about how this was to be accomplished, much emphasis was placed on the belief that both French and English-speaking Canadians would welcome Americans as liberators. The small number of British regular soldiers in Canada would be overwhelmed by American patriots, however inexperienced. The war was to be a coming-of-age ritual allowing a new generation of Americans to display their manliness.

U.S. Reenactors have a quiet moment before "The First Siege of Fort Meigs." [Nick Lachance]

History

The man selected to command the vital Northeast theatre of war stretching from Buffalo to the New England coast, Henry Dearborn, shared none of the optimism and enthusiasm of the Warhawks. Dearborn had fought in the Revolutionary War and had been captured at the siege of Québec in 1776. After he was exchanged for a British captive, Dearborn fought with distinction and joined Washington's staff in 1781. He served as Secretary of War in Jefferson's administration and retired to become Collector of Customs in Boston in 1809.

General Henry Dearborn. [G. Steuart]

Dearborn is usually written off as an aging incompetent plagued by indecision. Derided as "Granny Dearborn," he is said to have failed to provide the kind of leadership required to achieve victory in 1812 or 1813. It is, however, possible to look at Dearborn as a realist among dreamers. As Secretary of War he had presided over the reduction and reorganization of the army including the abolition of the office of Quartermaster General. He was well aware that under his successor, William Eustis, the War Office was understaffed and poorly organized, reliant upon civilian contractors for food, clothing, and equipment. He also knew that the regular Army, the only force that might be capable of confronting British professionals, had an effective strength of less than 7,000 men, many of them in the south or in posts on the frontier. Congress had authorized an "additional army" of 25,000 men in January 1812 but enlistment was slow and training barely begun. As late as November 1812 only 9,823 new recruits had enlisted.

Dearborn and other experienced officers on both sides of the border also understood the logistical challenges that armies faced when waging war in the borderland region. There were few roads and even fewer going in the right direction. Rivers and lakes provided the only effective means of transporting heavy artillery and bulk supplies. Dearborn also understood the tactical challenges facing the soldiers. The smooth-bore muskets available were only marginally more effective than those of the War of Independence. Firing at ranges over 150 yards were unlikely to produce more than 5% casualties or as one observer wrote, "a soldier must be very unfortunate indeed who shall be wounded by a common musket at 150 yards... as to firing at a man at 200... you may as well fire at the moon." Closing to less than 100 yards provided a much better chance of inflicting casualties so long as the weather was dry, the smoke of battle thinned by the breeze, and the percentage of misfires no higher than the normal one-in-six. Soldiers carried just sixty rounds of ammunition, further limiting their combat power.

Only the best disciplined troops could maintain a double line of infantry standing shoulder to shoulder at close range. The hastily recruited militia and semi-trained regular battalions available to the Americans in 1812 were simply no match for British professional soldiers though in time they too could learn the techniques of combat including the bayonet charge required in all successful battles.

The Americans and British would also employ artillery, guns, and howitzers on the battlefield. Both sides used the weight of the projectile to categorize their guns as three, six, 12, or 24-pounders. Roundshot cannon balls were commonly used though canisters filled with lead were also employed. Guns fired in a straight line. Howitzers used at shorter range lobbed their fused shell in an arc. Both weapons were smooth-bored and wildly inaccurate but could cause terrible casualties at close range.

The problem with artillery was transport and supply. If the Americans were to invade Canada they would have to bring their field artillery, six-pounder guns, with them. Each weighed – with carriage – close to 3,000 pounds and required teams of horses, as did the ammunition travelling in specially designed wagons or "caissons." To move the six guns of an American battery north over rough roads (better described as trails) was no easy task but without artillery, even hastily fortified positions could not be successfully attacked. Fixed artillery played a key role in repelling attacks but was far less effective in offensive operations.

Dearborn did not believe that the various state militias could provide an effective means of conquering Canada but under pressure from the President he authorized a three-pronged invasion of Canada with advances from Detroit, Buffalo, and Albany. If an attack from Detroit could be coordinated with an advance on Montréal and an assault across the Niagara River, the

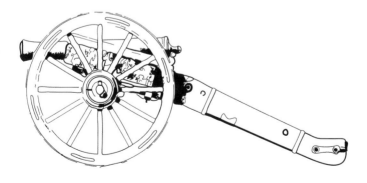

An illustration of a six-pounder that would have been used by both sides during the War of 1812.
[LCMSDS Illustration]

British might be stretched beyond the breaking point. Perhaps problems with manpower, logistics, divided command, and poor leadership could be overcome by simply marching north!

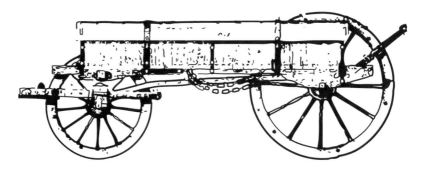

An illustration of the specially designed wagons called "caissons" that were used to move ammunition over long distances. [LCMSDS Illustration]

British Strategy

The United States declared war to force the repeal of the Orders-in-Council restricting trade, the impressment of American citizens, and to bring a halt to British support for First Nations resistance to American expansion. Despite their preoccupation with the Duke of Wellington's campaign in Spain and Napoleon's march on Moscow, the British cabinet sought to avoid war by repealing the Orders-in-Council, avoiding open clashes over impressments, and reducing support for First Nations warriors in the Northwest.

If war could not be avoided, the British Empire planned to stand defensively and avoid operations that might serve to unite American public opinion behind the war. The "Captain-General and Governor in Chief" of British North America, Sir George Prévost, understood that the preservation of Québec, the only permanent fortress in North America, was the key strategic objective and the "entry door" for any future mission to defend or recover the British colonies. Prévost was not opposed to limited operations to frustrate American initiatives if war broke out but he was nervous about the impact of frontier war on American public opinion. Even after war was declared he urged Major-General Isaac Brock, the military commander and acting Lieutenant-Governor in Upper Canada, to follow "extreme moderation in the use of the Indians, and to keep them in control as much as possible." In a July letter to Brock, almost a month after the outbreak of war, Prévost wrote:

> I consider it prudent and politic to avoid any measure which can in its effect have a tendency to unite the people in the American states. While

Sir Isaac Brock.
[C. Powell, LAC R11188-16-8-E]

Sir George Prévost.
[LAC 1948-125]

History

dissention prevails among them, their attempts on these provinces will be feeble…

British strategic planning also had to take into account the uncertain loyalties of the residents of the two Canadas. Prévost had worked hard to conciliate the clerical and political elites of French Canada who had been neglected and distrusted by his predecessor, Sir James Craig. By dispensing patronage and supporting the claims of the Roman Catholic hierarchy, Prévost had ended what French-Canadians called "Craig's Reign of Terror" but this did not mean the ordinary citizens had warm feelings for British officials or military officers. The first attempt to call out the militia resulted in protest and a violent confrontation in Lachine, a village on the Île de Montréal.

This situation in Upper Canada was equally uncertain. The majority of the population, estimated at 75,000 to 90,000, were so-called "later Loyalists;" individuals who had come to Canada from the United States since the 1790s in search of free land. They and their Loyalists counterparts lived a life of hardship and labour, clearing fields and striving to wrest a meagre living from their farms. Just 5% of the population lived in the three main villages. Kingston claimed 1,000 people and a number of stone buildings. "Muddy York" was home to 600 scattered along the shore west of the Don River. Newark or Niagara, with a population of 900, was the centre of the most prosperous region in the colony. The Grand River Valley was a reserve for those members of the Six Nations Iroquois Confederacy who had followed Joseph Brant north in 1783. Between the Grand and Detroit Rivers, scattered frontier settlements clung close to the lake with untouched forests and trackless swamps inland. The villages of Sandwich and Amherstburg in the far west were home to a mainly French Canadian population which was also the largest element in the villages across the river in Michigan.

Events of the American Revolution showed that the Maritime colonies of New Brunswick and Nova Scotia, while relatively safe from an attack over land, were vulnerable to an attack by sea. A program of fortifications along the coast was undertaken to rectify these weaknesses, principally in Saint John. Saint John was strategically situated at the mouth of the St. John River which was the only line of communication to the Canadas from Great Britain during the winter months when ice closed the St. Lawrence to navigation. The St. John River valley also contained significant timber resources, a strategic resource in the age of sail, crucial for the Royal Navy. Prévost's rapprochement with the French Canadian clerics and elites had already paid a dividend before the war broke out in the form of a tour to rally the support of the francophone Acadian communities of New Brunswick by Catholic Bishop Joseph Octave-Plessis. Simultaneous efforts were undertaken to

Fort Howe, overlooking the mouth of the St. John River, was constructed during the American Revolution to protect the inner harbour. [LAC PA-031720]

secure the neutrality of the local First Nations to help ensure that the war would be a quiet one in the Maritimes, at least on land.

The British were aware of the lack of support for war in the New England states as well as the Maritimes' dependence on food imports from New England. As a result, while the British were prepared to engage in a blockade of American trade they wanted to encourage New England trade with the Maritimes either through granting licences or encouraging smuggling into "freeports," ports of entry without import duties, such as St. Andrews, St. George, and Saint John. Despite this approach, both British and American privateers were active in the Gulf of Maine and Bay of Fundy area.

A wiser man than Madison might have postponed the declaration of war until his armies were ready to carry out a coordinated offensive. As it was, the only troops available to enter Canada in the summer of 1812 were General William Hull's "Army of the Northwest" at Detroit. This composite force consisted of the 4th Infantry Regiment of the Regular Army and three regiments of militia raised in Ohio. They had assembled at Dayton on 1 June and begun a 200 mile trek through wilderness and the Black Swamp, a 40 mile-wide wilderness that stretched from Lake Erie to Fort Wayne. Building a road as they advanced, Hull's men feared the vulnerability of their supply line erecting blockhouses that might offer some protection from hostile warriors.

Hull, who had been Governor of Michigan territory since 1805, had warned Washington that unless the United States seized control of Lake Erie by building warships superior to those of Britain's Provincial Marine, Detroit and the more remote forts at Mackinac Island and Dearborn (Chicago)

American Capture of Sandwich, 1812

History

could not be defended. No action was taken to build such a navy and as war fever swept Congress, Hull suggested that unless a force adequate to the defence of Detroit was dispatched immediately "it is more expedient to leave Michigan to its fate."

A well-trained, well-led force of 2,000 men might well have proved sufficient to protect Detroit and advance into Canada, but Hull's army was crippled by rivalries between militia and regulars, limited supplies, poor leadership, and exaggerated fears of First Nations warriors. After an unopposed crossing of the Detroit

General William Hull. [J. Sharples Sr. National Parks Service. NHP INDE 11911]

River on 12 July, Hull established his headquarters at Sandwich (Windsor), and issued a proclamation which promised to free the Canadian people from British tyranny and protect their "persons, property, and rights" so long as they remained in their houses. However:

> If contrary to your own interests and the expectation of my country, you should take part in the approaching contest, you will be considered and treated as enemies… If the barbarous and savage policy of Great Britain has pursued and the savages let loose to murder our citizens and butcher

The First Shot in the War of 1812 painted in 1909. [LC-USZ62-82749]

In a typical display of the exaggerated ferocity of Native warriors, this 1812 political cartoon alludes to the scalping of Americans at the behest of the British. The lines at the bottom read: "Arise Columbia's Sons and forward press, / Your Country's wrongs call loudly for redress; / The Savage Indian with his Scalping knife, / Or Tomahawk may seek to take your life; / By bravery aw'd they'll in a dreadful Fright, / Shrink back for Refuge to the Woods in Flight; / Their British leaders then will quickly shake, / And for those wrongs shall restitution make."
[William Charles, LC-DIG-ppmcsa-31111]

our women and children, this war will be a war of extermination… No white man found fighting by the side of an Indian will be taken prisoner. Instant destruction will be his lot.

The proclamation also invited the inhabitants of the region to join the American cause by volunteering their services to assist his army.

Few openly sided with the invaders but, after news of the proclamation spread, most of the Essex and Kent Militia mustered in accordance with the Militia Act returned to their homes to await events. Hull's army was now confronted with the task of capturing Fort Malden at Amherstburg before British reinforcements arrived. Ohio Militia under Colonel Lewis Cass seized the bridge that crossed Canard Creek four miles from the Fort but Hull refused to reinforce this detachment, believing that British control of the river and his own lack of artillery made the advance too dangerous.

Hull proposed to wait until mobile carriages for his 24-pounder guns were constructed and an alternate route to Fort Malden, away from the river, was available. No such road existed and building one was beyond the army's resources so the Americans remained at Sandwich, quarrelling among themselves. News of the fall of the Fort at Mackinac Island reached Hull on 29 July, leading him to believe that many more First Nations warriors would rally to the British cause. He requested large reinforcements and provisions, reporting that the Army's rations would only last another twenty days. An attempt to resupply the Army of the Northwest was already underway and Hull sent a small force south to escort the packhorses to Detroit. Major Thomas Van Horne's troops marched into a carefully prepared warrior ambush at Brownstown and were forced to retreat.

This skirmish and rumours of the dispatch of a large force of British troops from Niagara persuaded Hull to order a withdrawal to Detroit. He was later to tell his court-martial that "if I had attacked Malden, and had been successful it would have been a useless waste of blood. It would have been impossible to have maintained the fortress. It must have fallen for want of supplies."

Hull now proposed to withdraw the army to Maumee Rapids where it could be readily supported but the Ohio Militia Colonels refused to consider a retreat, accusing Hull of cowardice. Instead, a body of regulars and militia over six hundred strong, were sent up to link up with the supply column. A joint British and First Nations force at the village of Mahnaga barred the way but this time the Americans prevailed and the British withdrew. Despite this tactical victory no further advance was attempted and the packtrain was ordered to try and reach Detroit by an in-land route. On 13 August, Brock with 300 reinforcements reached Fort Malden and the initiative passed to the British. The first American offensive operation of the war had ended in failure.

A depiction of the famous meeting between Tecumseh and Brock at Fort Malden in August of 1812. This artistic representation is wholly invented and there is no historical evidence to substantiate this romanticized version. [LAC C-073719]

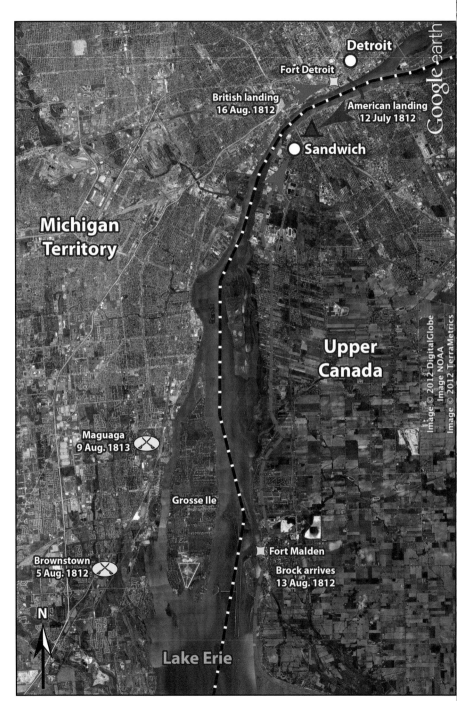

The Capture of Detroit, 1812

Operations in the Northwest, 1812

Brock learned at Amherstburg, through letters and dispatches from Hull and his unhappy subordinates captured at Brownstown, of a crisis in enemy morale and food shortages. The information led Brock to decide on immediate action. A meeting with Tecumseh and a council of First Nations leaders solidified an alliance especially after Brock outlined plans for an attack on Fort Detroit. Colonel Henry Proctor with 250 regulars, 50 Royal Newfoundland Fencibles, 400 militia, and 600 First Nations warriors were to cross the river and lure the Americans out of their fortifications. With just five small portable field artillery pieces and three larger guns, located across from Detroit, an assault on the fort by a numerically inferior force would be a very risky proposition.

Brock, who understood his enemy's fears, began the operation with a summons to surrender. "It is far from my intention," he declared, "to join in the war of extermination: but you must be aware that the numerous body of Indians who have attached themselves to my troops, will be beyond my control the moment the contest commences." Hull initially rejected the offer, but when the troops under Proctor and the warriors crossed the river the Americans withdrew into Fort Detroit. At 10:00 on 16 August, Hull raised a white flag and asked for negotiations leading to a surrender. The articles of capitulation were quickly agreed to and Brock took possession of the fort and all its arms and stores. The Ohio and Michigan Militia were paroled but Hull, his staff, and the officers in the U.S. regular army became prisoners of war to be transported to Québec until they were exchanged.

Brock, imitating Hull's earlier action, issued a proclamation announcing that not just Detroit but the "Territory of Michigan" had been "ceded to the arms of His Britannic Majesty." He promised to respect private property and maintain existing laws "until his Majesty's pleasure be known." The proclamation was unauthorized as well as unwise and simply angered American opinion.

A depiction of Hull's surrender in August of 1812.

Hull's surrender and Brock's proclamation sent a shockwave through the American frontier and the cities of the East. No one had anticipated the surrender of Detroit and Madison, who was in the midst of his re-election campaign, was outraged by what he saw as Hull's treachery. Within a few days, the news of the massacre of the garrison from Fort Dearborn was circulated and aroused intense hatred for First Nations warriors. Under instructions from Hull, Fort Dearborn had been abandoned and its small force of regulars and militia with 27 women and children had set out for Fort Wayne. Of the 67 soldiers and 27 dependents, 53 were killed and many of the rest wounded when hundreds of Potawatomi warriors attacked the column. Americans had lost control of the Northwest but the First Nations would now face American armies bent on revenge.

Brock promptly left for the Niagara frontier, his head full of plans for destroying the American base at Sackets Harbor and winning control of the Niagara region. As an operational commander he was disappointed to learn that Prévost and Dearborn had, on receipt of the news that the British Orders-in-Council had been repealed, agreed to a truce. Proctor, left in command at Detroit, was told to postpone the planned advance to Fort Wayne and to "restrain the Indians in their predatory excursions."

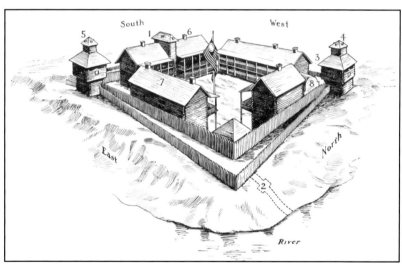

Fort Dearborn from *The Story of Old Fort Dearborn* as depicted in a drawing of a model by Albert Van den Berghenin in 1898 that appeared in the Chicago Daily Tribune on 5 March 1899.

Neither Proctor nor Tecumseh proved able to stem these "excursions" and the American settlements in Michigan were attacked and vandalized. Other groups of warriors made assaults against settlements in Indiana, but without artillery forts could not be taken so the warriors sought British support. In mid-September Proctor, ignoring Prévost's directions to remain on the defensive, sent an expedition to Fort Wayne under Captain Adam Muir.

Brock and Proctor argued that the advance into Indiana was undertaken to prevent another massacre, but Brock was fully aware of the consequences of his initiatives. He informed Prévost that First Nations had "heard of the armistice… and had we refused to joining them in the expedition it is impossible to calculate the consequences. I have already been asked to pledge my word that England would enter no negotiations in which their interests are not consulted." He warned Prévost "that should we desert them the consequences must be fatal."

There was little Prévost could do about the actions of his subordinates. In a letter to Brock he outlined his concerns but issued no new orders. He wrote:

Our numbers would not justify offensive operations being undertaken, unless they were solely calculated to strengthen a defensive attitude – I consider it prudent and polite to avoid any measure which can in its effect have a tendency to unite the people in the American States. Whilst dissention prevails among them, their attempts on these, Provinces will feeble; it is therefore our duty carefully to avoid committing any act which may, even by construction, tend to unite the Eastern and Southern States, unless by its perpetration we are to derive a considerable and important advantages.

The cover art of the "Fort Harrison March" musical score used in the Presidential Campaign of Zachary Taylor in 1848. The artistic piece portrays the defence of Fort Harrison and the elimination of the "aboriginal threat" to the Indiana Territory. In the American literature, it is depicted as the first U.S. land victory in the War of 1812. This is somewhat misleading given it was at best a defensive victory and Native Americans had little hope of capturing American forts without British support, particularly the need for the two-pounder.

A new American army was forming at Cincinnati when news of the fall of Detroit and the siege of Fort Wayne reached Harrison. The new army of the Northwest began their march at the end of August and as they approached Fort Wayne the warriors fled. Harrison continued north, burning First Nations villages and destroying crops. Before attempting to retake Detroit, Harrison sought permission to extend his campaign to the rest of Indiana. The Secretary of War replied that "Miamis as well as other Indians must be dealt with as their merits and demerits may in your judgment require." Troops acting under Harrison's orders returned to the Tippecanoe River, destroying everything in their path until an ambush at Wild Cat Creek, known as Spur's Defeat, and the weather forced a retreat. Harrison had also ordered an attack on villages along the Mississinewa River. After a forced march through December, the combination of warrior counterattacks and frostbite put an end to this enterprise.

While these punitive expeditions were underway, Harrison prepared for an advance to Detroit by three columns that were to converge at the rapids of the Maumee River where a base with a store of one million rations and other supplies was to be established. Nothing went according to plan and one column of troops under General James Winchester nearly mutinied as starvation, autumn rains, and disease sapped morale. News that the British were seizing stores of beef, corn, and wheat at Frenchtown (Monroe) on the River Raisin led Winchester to send a regiment of Kentucky Militia to the site.

The Americans attacked 18 January, routing the small British foraging party. They occupied Frenchtown, apparently convinced that their position was secure. Proctor gathered his forces for an immediate counterattack arriving at Frenchtown at dawn on 22 January. With his regulars in the centre and warriors on either flank, Proctor began the action relying on his light artillery. The regulars made slight progress but their action fixed American attention allowing the warriors to harass and then overrun their flanks. The character of the war between the Americans and the First Nations was quickly evident as no quarter was given. Winchester was captured and brought before Proctor who urged him to surrender. Terms were negotiated including the protection of prisoners and private property. The British withdrew, taking their seriously wounded in the available sleighs and the walking wounded of both armies. Proctor refused to leave an armed guard behind though he knew this meant the wounded prisoners were unlikely to survive because he believed American reinforcements were close by. It was, he reported, "impossible to save any prisoner… where the Indians have lost lives." Total casualties at Frenchtown were horrendous. The Americans reported 397 killed and 547 taken prisoner – a 90% lost rate. The British casualties were 185 men or 40% of those engaged. No one recorded the fate of the First Nations warriors.

The second battle at the River Raisin completed the process of transforming the American image of the war into one in which they saw themselves as the victims of a cruel and merciless enemy, not the aggressors who had declared war and invaded Canada. The cry "Remember the Raisin" became an important tool in recruiting propaganda.

MASSACRE of the AMERICAN PRISONERS, at FRENCH-TOWN, on the River Raisin, by the SAVAGES Under the Command of the British Genl PROCTOR. January 23rd 1813

This propaganda image – "Massacre of the American Prisoners at Frenchtown on the River Raisin by the Savages under the command of the British General Proctor" – wrongly depicts a complicit British force during the slaughter. Regardless, the famous rallying call "Remember the Raisin" became an important piece of propaganda.

History

Lake Ontario, 1812

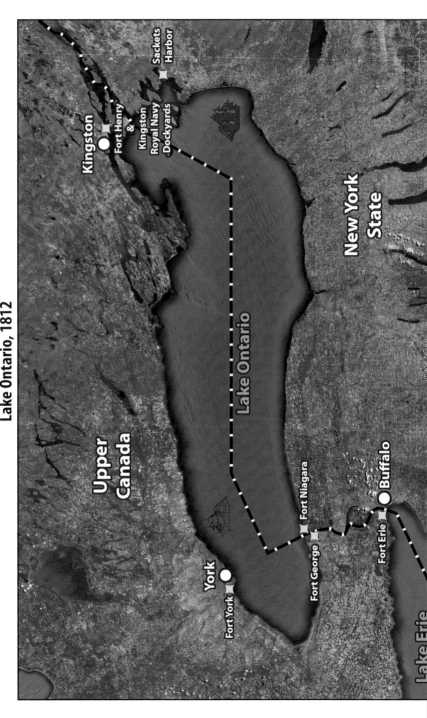

Queenston Heights, 1812

The confusion that characterized the efforts of the American armies in 1812 was especially evident on the northern frontier of New York State. General Dearborn did not seem to understand that his command extended to the shores of Lake Ontario and the Niagara. He focused energies on coastal defence and the logistical problems of an advance on Montréal from Albany and Lake Champlain, leaving western New York to the state militia.

One brigade of New York Militia was committed to the defence of the villages south of the St. Lawrence at the eastern end of Lake Ontario. A British attempt to destroy the American warship *Oneida* at Sackets Harbor in July drew attention to the area. Captain Benjamin Forsyth and a company of regulars joined General Jacob Brown's militia at the naval base. In September, Forsyth launched a raid across the river seizing provisions, arms, and ammunition stored at Gananoque. Two weeks later, a large body of Canadian militia launched an attack on Ogdensburg but turned back in the face of strong American defences. Small, costly actions at the St. Regis Reserve and French Mills (Fort Covington) added to border tension but neither side had the resources or the will to attempt to occupy territory. If the conquest of Canada was to happen in 1812, the obvious place to attack in strength was across the Niagara River.

By October more than 6,000 American troops including 3,000 regulars were encamped at Fort Niagara, Lewiston, and Buffalo. Dearborn instructed

The interior of Fort Niagara. [Lossing]

History

Initial Stages of the Battle of Queenston Heights, 1812

the commander of the New York Militia, Major-General Stephen Van Rensselaer, to "embrace the first practical opportunity for effecting a forward movement" on the assumption that all the American forces in the area would come under his command. Van Rensselaer had no military experience and was reliant on his cousin, a former regular officer and veteran of the Battle of Fallen Timbers, for advice. The senior regular officer at Niagara, General Alexander Smyth, was so contemptuous of the militia and Van Rensselaer that he kept his men apart and refused to attend the planning conference that preceded the attack.

Brock leaving Niagara. [Arthur Hider, LAC C-046958]

Divided command, poor discipline, restless troops prone to desert; all this was a recipe for disaster. The first attempt to cross the river failed when it was discovered that oars for the boats had disappeared, "due to treason, fear, or mere incompetence." Two nights later, small groups of American troops crossed the river at Queenston following a fisherman's path to reach the heights. The Americans captured the redan battery that was supposed to control the river and kept adding men to their position on the high ground.

Brock had organized the Niagara defences placing detachments close to the likely crossing places especially Fort George and Fort Erie. The American force on Queenston Heights might be a diversion and Brock decided to counterattack. Historian George Stanley describes what happened:

> The Americans held the Heights and the bulk of the British troops were still on the march from Fort George to Queenston. Perhaps he should have waited, but boldness in action was the very nature of the man. Any delay would serve the purposes of the Americans more than his own. He was not ready to allow the enemy to seize the initiative, not if he could keep it for himself.
>
> Two months before, at Detroit, Brock had said that he would never ask men to go 'where I do not lead them.' Wholly disregarding the danger of such a course of action, he led his men on foot up the hill, on the double. The first charge was shattered by the intensity of Wool's fire; one participant called it 'a most galling fire.' Even the grenadiers began to falter. Brock rallied them with the shout, 'This is the first time I have ever seen the 49th turn their backs.' The men picked up the challenge, and with Brock in his red tunic well ahead of them, brandishing his sword, slipping

History

Final Stages of the Battle of Queenston Heights, 1812

and stumbling in the wet grass, the charge went on. At about 50m Brock cried to his men to hold their fire and use the bayonet. A short distance away, from behind a clump of bushes, an American scout raised his long rifle and, taking careful aim, sent a musket ball tearing into Brock's chest, just above the heart. [...]

Brock's aide, John Macdonell, tried to retrieve the situation. He collected about fifty men, including some of the 49th and a few York militia, and attempted another dash towards the battery. But the determination of the original charge was lacking. The Americans were ready and waiting at 30 metre range. According to one of the survivors: 'Lieutenant Colonel Macdonell, who was on the left of our party calling up on us to advance, received a shot in his body and fell. His horse was at the same instant killed. Captain Williams, who was at the other extremity of out little band, fell the next moment, apparently dead.'

Macdonell, mortally wounded, was carried back to the village by another militia officer who had been at Brown's Point. There was little more the British could do. Wool's undetected clamber up the cliff and the single shot of a sniper had turned the battle from probable defeat to possible victory for the Americans. And Issac Brock died a soldier's death, just three days after his elevation to the rank of Knight of the Bath by George III. It was his reward for the victory at Detroit, an honour he never knew he had received.

The Battle for Queenston Heights 13 October 1812. [John Kelly, LAC C-000273]

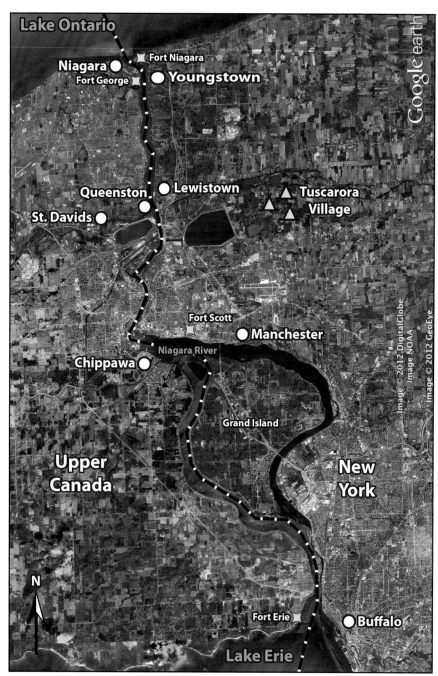

Niagara Region, 1812

After Macdonell was killed, the surviving senior officer, Captain James Denis, ordered a withdrawal to await the arrival of the much larger contingent from Fort George. Major-General Roger Sheaffe, an unpopular but competent officer, made the decision to circle around Queenston to gain the heights without having to fight uphill. A party of Mohawk warriors from Grand River under Captain John Norton and the Lincoln Militia, which included a company of Black volunteers, supported the 49th British Regiment as it advanced on the enemy position.

The systematic advance of Sheaffe's force of red-coated regulars and militia seems to have panicked many of the Americans who fled the battlefield seeking refuge by re-crossing the river or hiding along its banks. Lieutenant-Colonel Winfield Scott and a small band of regulars fought on until they

An artistic representation of Richard Pierpoint during the War of 1812. The 'Coloured Corps' fought alongside Brock at Queenston Heights and for the duration of the war. Each soldier was awarded 100 acres of land when peace was signed in 1815. [Canadian War Museum]

were surrounded and forced to surrender. American accounts of the battle focus on the failure of the New York Militia to reinforce their comrades at Queenston. According to Van Rensselaer:

> …at the very moment when complete victory was in our hands the ardour of the unengaged troops had entirely subsided. Whether the severity of the first action – the name of Indians – or the sight of some wounded intimidated them I cannot say… My whole camp was full of men, not a company, scarcely a man could be persuaded to turn his face to the river…

The difficulty with this interpretation is that it fails to explain why a force of over 1,000 men holding a position that had time to organize collapsed in a few hours when confronted with an army of roughly equal size. There was not much point in sending more militia across unless they had the will to fight. More than 900 soldiers surrendered to Sheaffe, suggesting a total collapse of morale.

Van Rensselaer resigned leaving the Niagara frontier to the posturing of Alexander Smyth who claimed that he would redeem the failures of leadership that had led to the defeat at Queenston Heights. On 19 November, several companies of American troops crossed the Niagara River near Buffalo establishing a shallow bridgehead. A second group was met by heavy fire and was unable to land. The next morning, Smyth began to embark his main force. It was raining heavily in close to freezing temperatures and Smyth decided to reconsider. He called a council of his officers and asked them: "Is it expedient to cross over now? and is the force we have sufficient to conquer the opposite coast." There was no agreement on what to do and the action was postponed until the next day then postponed again. The American camp was soon in

The Port of Buffalo 1813. [Lossing]

chaos. "Troops milled around firing their muskets in all directions…" Smyth went into hiding, only emerging to fight a duel with the New York Militia General Peter Porter. Firing at 12 paces they both missed. The American "Army of the Center" disintegrated and Smyth's name was struck off the rolls of the U.S. Army. The worst was yet to come. The remains of the American army went into winter quarters at Buffalo where poor sanitation, inadequate food and clothing, and a typically cold, snowy winter were responsible for the deaths of 300, far more than had fallen in battle.

The Brock Memorial in 2012, Queenston Heights, Ontario. [Matt Symes]

Lake Champlain and the St. Lawrence, 1812

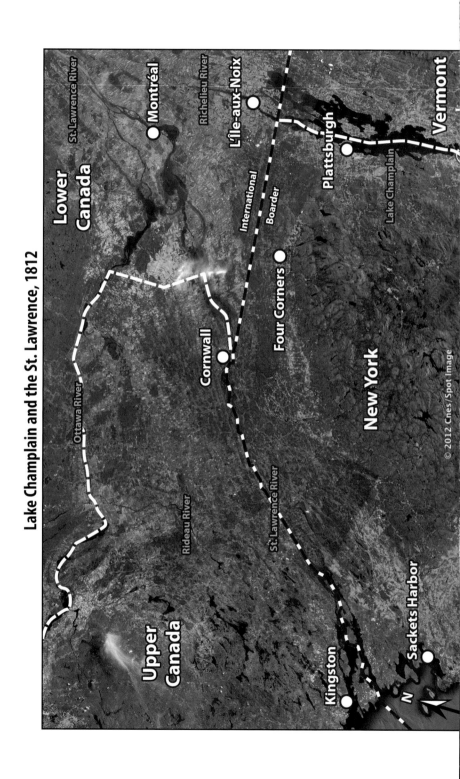

The Lake Champlain Frontier, 1812

In response to a direct order from the Secretary of War, General Dearborn began to move the army he had assembled at Albany to Plattsburgh in November. By then Hull had surrendered Detroit and Van Rensselaer had resigned in disgrace after Queenston Heights. It is therefore not surprising that Dearborn, who had little confidence in his untrained, poorly disciplined troops, was reluctant to begin an advance on Montréal. His northern army of 6,000 men was made up of recently recruited regulars and short-term militia from New York and New England, many of whom had already given notice that they had agreed to serve in defence of their country, not to invade Canada.

Dearborn was also concerned with the challenges presented by the battle space and the ways in which the British had taken advantage of it. The best way into Canada was via the Richelieu River which was navigable as far as the rapids at St. Jean. Prévost appointed Major-General Francis de Rottenburg, a Swiss-born professional soldier, to command the defences south of Montréal, and his first task was to rebuild the neglected fortifications along the Richelieu at Île-aux-Noix, St. Jean, and Chambly.

Something might have been accomplished if Dearborn had been able to act promptly in the summer of 1812, but by November Île-aux-Noix was too strong to attack. This left the overland route from Plattsburgh to the south shore of the St. Lawrence opposite Montréal as the best option. Dearborn believed that there was little point in advancing to Montréal without substantial reinforcements. His army, he insisted, needed better

Île-aux-Noix, Québec. [Parks Canada]

logistical backup and 3,000 additional regular troops if Montréal was to be held through the winter. He told the Secretary of War that he "could not consent to crossing the St. Lawrence with the uncertainty of being able to remain there."

There was little chance of obtaining such troops after the disasters in the Northwest and Niagara and Dearborn was determined to avoid another crushing defeat. Intelligence reports suggested that de Rottenburg deployed roughly 1,200 regulars and 1,500 "well-disciplined militia" south of Montréal as well as "about 300 Indians." Dearborn ordered a reconnaissance-in-strength with 500 men of the 11th and 15th Infantry Regiments commanded by Colonel Zebulon Pike, the famous explorer who was an experienced officer. Their task was to eliminate the threat posed by a band of First Nations warriors said to be lying in wait. After a careful search failed to discover any warriors, Pike decided to continue north and seized the only fortification in the area, the blockhouse at the village of Lacolle.

Pike organized a bayonet charge to achieve surprise but when the garrison opened fire, the inexperienced regulars lost all cohesion and more Americans were wounded by friendly fire then by the British. The confused fire fight ended when the blockhouse caught fire and the garrison withdrew. Pike and his men returned to Champlain ready to lead the army north the next morning. It was not to be. Most of the New York and Vermont Militia refused to cross the border. The small naval force available was unable to bypass Île-aux-Noix and there was no prospect of additional regular troops. The militia soldiers manned the border posts or were sent home, the regulars went into winter quarters. Before spring, more than 100 of them died of disease and were buried at Plattsburgh.

A 1920s image of the blockhouse at Lacolle. [Government of Ontario]

A merican strategy at the outbreak of war was based on the belief that the conquest of Canada would force the British Empire to negotiate an honourable peace resolving the issue of impressment, illegal blockades, the British Order-in-Council against neutral trade and alleged British support of the First Nations in the Northwest frontier. Instead, though by 1813 impressment remained unresolved, the failed campaigns of 1812 had strengthened British and Canadian resolve and re-ignited a war with the First Nations. The Madison administration could claim success at sea, where in a series of single-ship actions American frigates had triumphed, but these tactical victories resulted in an intensified British blockade of the eastern seaboard that damaged the American economy. In the face of the intensified blockade the Americans increasingly relied on privateering to attack British trade. Despite American privateers being relatively successful in 1812 with over 200 vessels captured, the extension of the British blockade into the American littoral curtailed privateering. To make matters more

The artist gloats over naval losses suffered by England early in the War of 1812, in particular the defeat of the warship "Boxer" by the American frigate "Enterprise" in September 1813. King George III stands at left, his nose bleeding and eye blackened, saying, "Stop...Brother Jonathan, or I shall fall with the loss of blood -- I thought to have been too heavy for you -- But I must acknowledge your superior skill -- Two blows to my one! -- And so well directed too! Mercy, mercy on me, how does this happen!!!" On the right, his opponent James Madison says, "Ha-Ah Johnny! you thought yourself a "Boxer" did you! -- I'll let you know we are an "Enterprize"ing Nation and ready to meet you with equal force any day." In the background, on the ocean, two ships are engaged in battle. [William Charles, LC-DIG-ppmsca-10754]

History

difficult, news of Napoleon's retreat from Moscow in November 1813 and the devastation of his army suggested that Britain would soon be able to send additional troops to North America. The situation led James Monroe, the Secretary of State, to suggest that it was time to make "an accommodation with Great Britain" but Madison knew that "Warhawk" congressmen and their constituents were determined to continue a war that was now more about recovering Michigan and eliminating the threat posed by the alliance of First Nations.

The results of the 1812 campaigns also affected British strategy. After Brock's proclamation extending the surrender of Detroit to all of Michigan, General Proctor proposed a far-reaching plan to extend British control to the vast Illinois territory and establish a quasi-sovereign First Nations territory jointly guaranteed by Britain and the United States. Surprisingly, the British government endorsed the idea, insisting that in any peace negotiations "the security of their (First Nations) possessions may not be compromised or forgotten."

This fundamental strategic conflict helps to explain the reluctance of both the British and Americans to actively pursue the Russian offer of mediation in early 1813. Although neither Madison nor the Warhawks yet knew that the British sought a permanent change in the balance of power in North America they were determined to regain full control of the Northwest before serious peace negotiations began. The key to victory in the west was control of Lake Erie, so while new armies assembled, the focus shifted to the lakes.

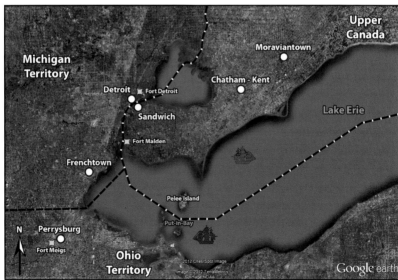

The Detroit Frontier, 1812

Operations, 1813

On 14 January 1813 the new American Secretary of War, John Armstrong, took office with plans to gain control of the Great Lakes in a series of operations against Kingston, Fort George, and Fort Erie. Kingston, Armstrong believed, was the key to unlocking the defences of Upper Canada as control of the town would cut supply lines and deny the British fleet a safe harbour. Armstrong ordered General Dearborn to assemble an army at Sackets Harbor and cooperate with the naval commander Captain Isaac Chauncey to attack Kingston as soon as the ice left the lake.

Captain Isaac Chauncey. [Gilbert Stuart]

This sensible plan offered the Americans the chance to win a decisive victory by cutting British supply lines, destroying most of the fleet and occupying their major naval base. Prévost was aware of the danger an attack on Kingston posed to the British position in Upper Canada and the need for reinforcements there. Prévost was limited to those already in North America since by the time the winter ice cleared from the St. Lawrence River it would be too late. The only option was for six companies of the 104th Regiment of Foot, then stationed in New Brunswick, to proceed up the St. John River by snowshoe and cross the grand portage to Rivière du Loup and

A photo of the colours of the 104th (New Brunswick) Regiment of Foot. [NB Museum]

March of the 104th (New Brunswick) Regiment of Foot, 1813

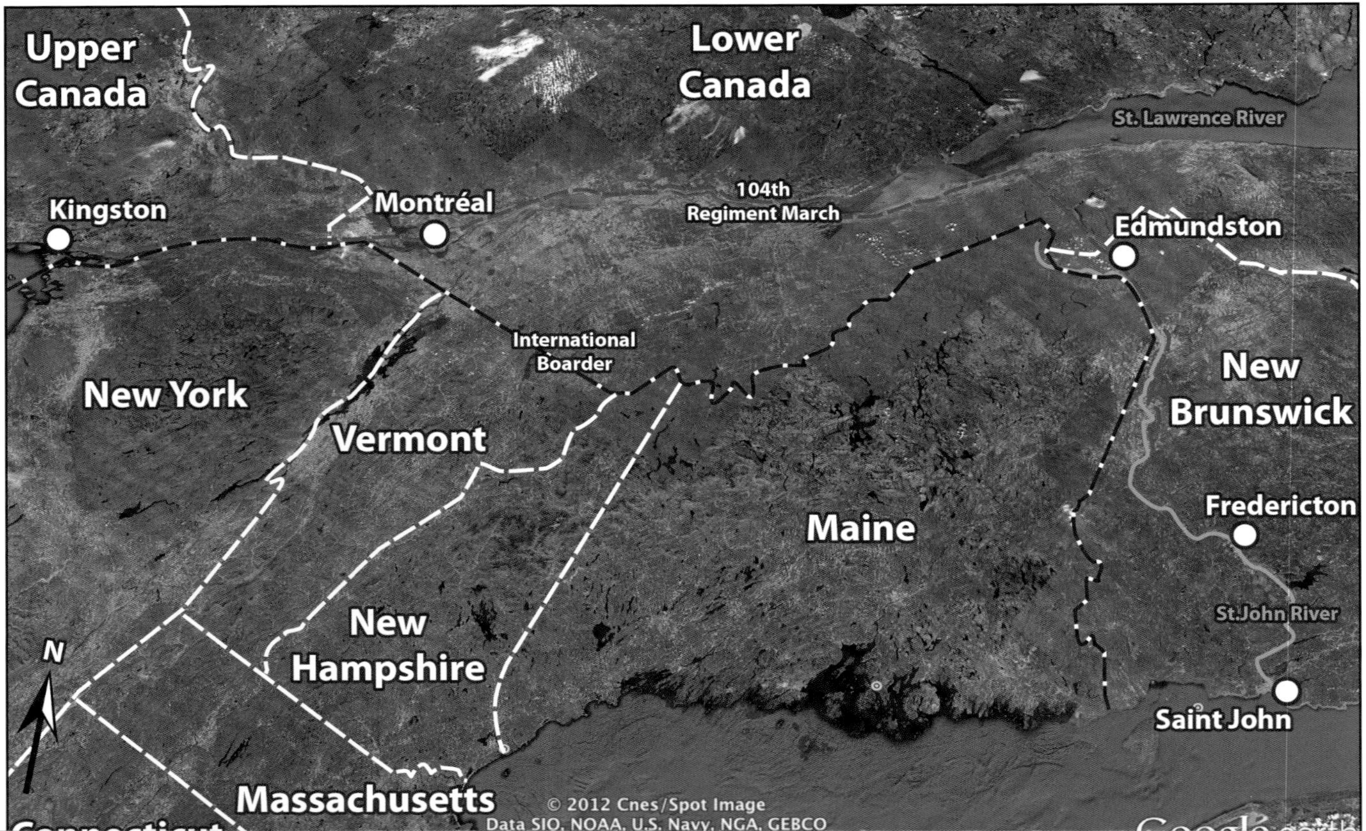

then proceed along the St. Lawrence to Kingston. The 104th began their over 1100km march on 16 February 1813 and with a short pause in Québec City attained Kingston on 12 April. Fortunately for the British, Dearborn relied on dubious intelligence and took council of his fears. Exaggerated reports of the number of reinforcements arriving in Kingston and news of the capture of Ogdensburg by Lieutenant-Colonel "Red George" Macdonell and his Glengarry Fencibles persuaded Dearborn that Kingston was too strongly defended, while York could be captured as a prelude to winning control of the Niagara Peninsula. Only then would Kingston be attacked.

Chauncey, a veteran naval officer, reached the same conclusion but for different reasons. He thought that the capture of Kingston would require a major effort and might take too much time. The main object of the campaign of 1813 was control of the Northwest and defeat of the First Nations. Chauncey believed that a combined operation at Niagara would produce an easy victory. It would also release the ships held at Black Rock by the guns of Fort Erie, allowing them to join the fleet at Presque Ile and win control of Lake Erie. Once the Americans dominated Lake Erie the British would have to abandon Fort Malden and the Southwestern part of the colony.

Chauncey had arrived at Sackets Harbor in October 1812 with two experienced sailors and a number of shipwrights. By the spring of 1813, his fleet was large enough to challenge the British for control of Lake Ontario. The operation to capture York and the ships in its harbour began on 26 April when Chauncey's 15 ships and 1,700 men of Dearborn's army arrived off Toronto Island. The next morning the Americans landed to the west of York and after skirmishes with First Nations warriors advanced on the town. The American fleet provided continuous support with its guns. The defenders,

A depiction of the Capture of Ogdensburg. Government buildings and some ships frozen in the ice were burned. The Americans did not replace the garrison at Ogdesnburg for the duration of the War of 1812, leaving the British supply route open. [Government of Canada]

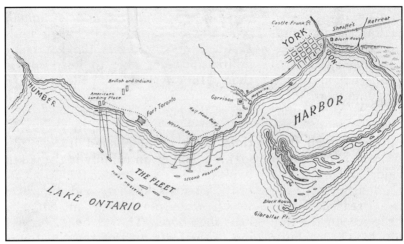

Map of York, 1813. [LAC e010963335]

600 men of the 8th (King's) Regiment and a company of Newfoundland Fencibles, were forced to retreat "against the greatly superior and increasing numbers of the enemy." A hastily organized defensive position at the Western Battery ended when the powder magazine blew up, killing 20 men.

Major General Sheaffe, who was in York in his role as civil administrator of Upper Canada, ordered his regular forces to disengage and begin a retreat to Kingston. The militia were told to surrender and obtain the best terms they could. Sheaffe ordered the destruction of all military supplies and the ship under construction at the dockyard. When the main magazine at Fort York exploded, debris struck nearby American troops, killing Zebulon Pike and

BURNING THE DON BRIDGE. TORONTO
– 1813 –
(From a sketch by Isaac Bellamy.)

Burning the Don Bridge, York, 1813. [LAC 1958-046]

37 of his soldiers. Over 200 others were wounded. The sudden, unexpected losses may explain the behaviour of poorly disciplined soldiers who looted the town and burnt its principal buildings.

The terms of capitulation included the customary means for paroling the militia who had surrendered. The British and United States governments had agreed to formalize the system in November 1812. Accurate lists of those captured and paroled were to be kept by both sides so that proper exchanges could be arranged and men on parole allowed to serve again. The Americans reported 241 militia taken prisoner at York, all of who were paroled and released the next day. News of the value of parole papers, allowing men to avoid militia service, especially during the crucial spring planting season, spread quickly. As many as 1,400 men from the area came to York to give themselves up and win parole. This behaviour outraged the Reverend John Strachan and the local grandees but it made perfect sense to men who knew that their families would suffer if they could not get crops into the ground. For the Americans, the loss of General Pike and other casualties, one fifth of their strength, and the failure to prevent Sheaffe from burning the frigate under construction before retreating to Kingston, limited the value of their first land victory of the war.

The death of U.S. General Pike at the Battle of York. [Canadian Military History Gateway, DND]

The Niagara Frontier, 1813

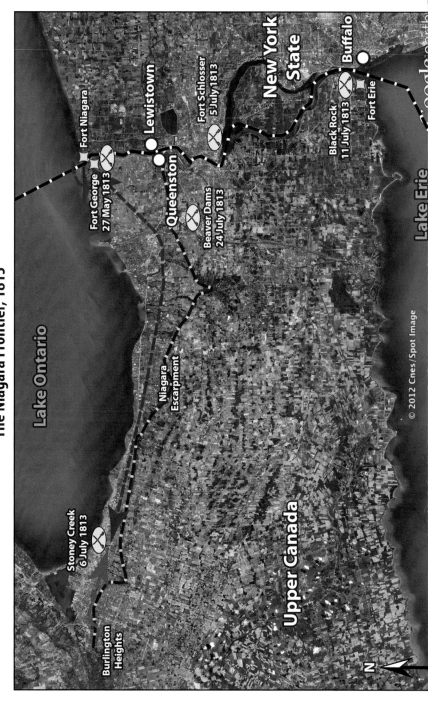

Lake Ontario

Lake Erie

New York State

Upper Canada

Stoney Creek
6 July 1813

Burlington
Heights

Niagara
Escarpment

Fort Niagara

Fort George
27 May 1813

Queenston

Beaver Dams
24 July 1813

Lewistown

Fort Schlosser
5 July 1813

Black Rock
11 July 1813

Buffalo

Fort Erie

© 2012 Cnes/Spot Image

N

The Niagara Frontier, 1813

The American fleet, with the regiments that fought at York on board, reached Niagara on 8 May but the fighting at York, storms on Lake Ontario, and sickness meant the men were in no condition to begin a new campaign. When additional troops ferried from Sackets Harbor arrived, General Dearborn and his new Chief of Staff, Winfield Scott, commanded 4,700 troops. Across the river Brigadier General John Vincent deployed 1,800 regulars, 500 militia, and 100 Mohawk warriors from Grand River. They garrisoned Fort George, a post at Chippawa and Fort Erie.

Mowhak Warrior. [Ronald B. Volstad DND]

Winfield Scott.

The presence of Chauncey's ships allowed Dearborn to execute a plan designed to outflank the British defences and land troops on the Lake Ontario shore. The decision to land at Two Mile Creek instead of further west made it possible for Vincent to disengage the bulk of his men and withdraw all the regulars and Mohawks to Beaver Dams and then Burlington Heights, abandoning the Niagara Peninsula but saving an army. The militia was told to return to their homes and apply for paroles. American records indicate that more than 1,000 parole applications were granted, double the number of men eligible for them. Local residents assumed that the British defeat and withdrawal meant the end of the war in the region. No one anticipated that conflict and indecision would slow the American pursuit and allow Vincent and his army to regain the initiative.

The detachments of Dearborn's army took six days to reach Stoney Creek where General John Chandler ordered his forces to encamp in preparation for an assault on Burlington Heights. His 2,500 man army composed of regular regiments was posted along the creek from the lakeshore to the escarpment.

History

Brigadier Vincent, a veteran officer who had served in Canada since 1802, was 49 years old in 1813. As garrison commander at Kingston he had organized the defence of the town when Chauncey's squadron pursued the Royal George and threatened an attack. Sent to Niagara to replace Major-General Sheaffe who was ill, Vincent appeared as unenthusiastic as the militia who he reported were all too ready to desert. Fortunately his senior staff officer, Lieutenant-Colonel John Harvey, was younger and far more aggressive. Harvey, who had made the overland trip from New Brunswick to Québec on snowshoes to take up his appointment as Deputy Adjutant General in Upper Canada, was to demonstrate his adventurous spirit throughout the balance of the war. He personally scouted the position, reporting that "the enemy guards were few and negligent, his line of encampment was long and broken, his artillery feebly supported…" Harvey urged an immediate attack and at 0200 hours on 6 June he led 750 officers and men of the 49th and King's Regiment into a night action. Initially surprise was achieved, but the Americans rallied and a confused battle erupted. American and British accounts of Stoney Creek seem to describe two different battles but during the night both American Generals – Chandler and his subordinate Brigadier William Winder – were captured. Leaderless and disorganized, the Americans retreated to Forty Mile Creek, a position they were forced to abandon when the British fleet appeared threatening their supply line.

The Battle of Stoney Creek. [C.W. Jeffrys]

Undated photo of the Battle of Stoney Creek Monument.

The arrival of Commodore James Yeo's fleet was an episode in a complex naval war that continued throughout 1813. Yeo, who served as commander-in-chief of the Royal Navy in the Canadas from May 1813 until the end of the war, had enlisted as a boy volunteer at age eleven. His first command was the French privateer *Confiance* which he captured in daring action. Appointed a Post Captain at age twenty-five, he led an Anglo-Portuguese expedition to capture Cayenne in French Guiana and was knighted by both Britain and Portugal. Yeo took command at Kingston on 15 May and by the end of the month was ready to organize an amphibious landing to destroy the dockyards and ships under construction at Sackets Harbor. The venture was made possible by the absence of Chauncey's fleet which was landing troops in the Niagara.

The battle for Sackets Harbor began on 28 May when a convoy of boats bringing reinforcements to the American garrison was intercepted. Mississauga and Mohawk warriors moving swiftly in canoes attacked the heavily-laden battleaux and after a bloody skirmish onshore the Americans raised a white flag, surrendering 115 men. Prévost, who was with Yeo's squadron, displayed his customary caution postponing an immediate attack much to the dismay of Yeo and the army officers.

James Yeo. [Lossing]

The Second Battle of Sackets Harbor, 1813

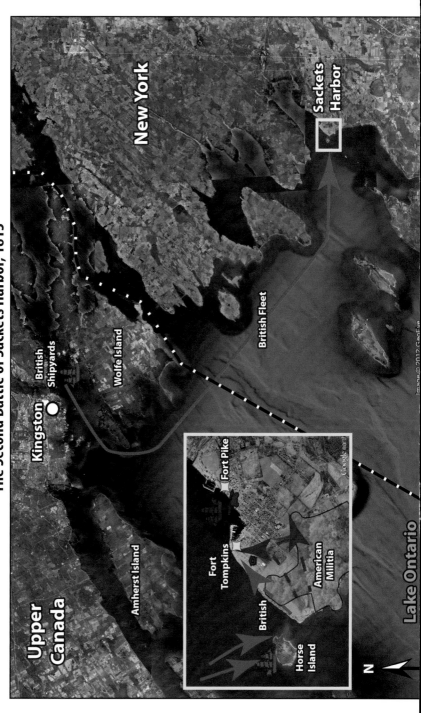

Sackets Harbor. [Lossing]

The next day the British and Canadians landed at Horse Island, advancing overland to the harbour. A confused and indecisive battle followed. As American resistance stiffened, Prévost ordered a withdrawal. The harbour had not been captured but a junior American officer, fearing the worst, had ordered the destruction on the sloop-of-war under construction as well as naval supplies. British losses were 30 killed and 200 wounded. The Americans suffered 153 casualties with 150 taken prisoner.

When news of the attack on his home base reached Chauncey he abandoned Dearborn's army, returning to Sackets Harbor. The British failed to capture their objective but a large quantity of naval stores had been destroyed before Yeo withdrew to Kingston. With Chauncey racing east, Yeo sailed west arriving off Niagara in time to harass the American troops retreating from Stoney Creek.

The Americans withdrew to Fort George where Dearborn composed a dispatch rationalizing his failure. The Secretary of War, John Armstrong, was not pleased. His reply to Dearborn commented on the "strange fatality attending our efforts" and expressed his surprise at the repeated escapes of the enemy. "Battles are not won," he noted, when "an inferior enemy is not destroyed." Dearborn's troubles were not over. The British followed the American retreat establishing a series of outposts which were used to harass the troops at Fort George. The new American commander, General John Boyd, described by his predecessor as "a compound of ignorance, vanity and petulance," agreed to a proposal to strike at one of the outposts near Beaver Dams, with a force of 575 men, including a company of light artillery and a troop of Dragoons. Laura Secord, the wife of a Lincoln militia sergeant wounded at Queenston Heights, overheard discussions about the raid and walked by a circuitous route of over twenty miles to warn the British. Lieutenant James FitzGibbon, who commanded the outpost with just 47 men, relied on a newly arrived company of warriors from St. Regis and

Deux Montagnes led by a French Canadian Militia officer, Dominique Ducharme, to ambush the Americans.

On 24 June, Ducharme and his men let the column pass then attacked from woods at the rear with musket fire and "war whoops." A three-hour battle developed but was ended after reinforcements reached Ducharme in the form of the Mohawks from Grand River led by Captain William Johnson Kerr. Lieutenant FitzGibbon also brought his men forward and under a flag of truce persuaded the Americans that a large British force was arriving and the warriors were seeking revenge for losses. Colonel Charles Boerstler agreed to surrender the 542 officers and men then under his command. FitzGibbon was lauded for his actions but his own report stated:

The Laura Secord monument at Drummond Hill Cemetery. [Niagara Falls Public Library 96251]

> … not a shot was fired by our side except by the Indians. They beat the American detachment into a state of terror, and the only share I claim is taking advantage of a favourable moment to offer them protection from the tomahawk and the scalping knife.

The Americans, who called Beaver Dams the Battle of the Beechwoods, were demoralized by yet another defeat and Armstrong used the incident to relieve Dearborn of his command. The British re-occupied Queenston, Chippawa, and Fort Erie while the Americans clung to Fort George, their only foothold on the Canadian side of the river.

Major-General de Rottenburg, who replaced Vincent in command at Burlington Heights, authorized an aggressive raiding policy. On 5 July Lieutenant-Colonel Thomas Clark, with a company of Lincoln Militia, crossed to Fort Schlosser, overcame the garrison and returned with arms and ammunition. A week later a much larger raid, commanded by Lieutenant-Colonel Cecil Bisshopp landed at Black Rock. They were able to destroy blockhouses, the naval yard and a schooner before the Americans counterattacked. The raiders returned with 123 barrels of salt and 46 barrels of whiskey, but Bisshopp and twelve of his men were killed.

British domination of Niagara ended after the defeat at Moraviantown. Sheaffe again withdrew to Burlington Heights on the assumption that Harrison's victorious army would continue east and cut off troops holding forward positions in the peninsula. Harrison, his own logistical arrangements at risk, declined the opportunity and sailed to Buffalo and then Sackets Harbor where his regular regiments were to join the planned advance on Montréal.

Beaver Dams Memorial. [Toronto Public Library, JRR 1345 Cab IV]

The temporary vacuum of power was filled by Joseph Willcocks and his Company of Canadian Volunteers formed from men who had chosen to side with the Americans. Willcocks had been a Member of the Upper Canada Assembly and leader of a group of MLAs who formed an opposition "party." They had prevented Brock from suspending habeas corpus in 1812 but, after the outbreak of war, had shown loyalty to the British or at least the Canadian cause. The decision of Willcocks and two of his assembly colleagues, Abraham Markle and Benjamin Mallory, to swear allegiance to the United States has been explained in terms of their opposition to arbitrary authority. This speculative view does nothing to explain Willcocks' role in leading a raiding force that harassed and plagued former neighbours, nor does it account for his personal role in the burning of Newark (Niagara-on-the-Lake) in December 1813.

This incident, one of the most pointless and destructive acts of the war, occurred after Lieutenant-Colonel John Murray with some 500 men returned to the Niagara frontier to counter Willcocks' raids. The American commander, Brigadier-General George McClure, fearing reprisals decided to abandon Fort George and agreed to Willcocks' proposal to burn Newark. McClure had been given the authority to burn the village only "if necessary to defend Fort George." This allowed the American government to disavow his action but in December 1813 this wanton terror inspired immediate revenge

History

Newark in Flames, 1813. [Lossing]

attacks by British forces. A new commander-in-chief, Lieutenant-General Sir Gordon Drummond, and a recently promoted Major-General, Phinias Riall, had arrived to take charge in Upper Canada and both men were eager to make their mark. Drummond appointed a commissioner to investigate persons suspected of treason that led to the trials known as the Ancaster "Bloody" Assize of 1814 when eight of the nineteen Canadians captured while involved in raids on Upper Canada were executed. Drummond reached Niagara in mid-December and after surveying the ruins of Fort George and Newark, ordered an immediate assault on Fort Niagara. Colonel John Murray, with more than 500 regulars, crossed the river on 19 December and stormed the fort, capturing 350 prisoners, cannons, muskets, and other stores worth around 150,000 pounds sterling which was distributed as prize money to the soldiers engaged in the action.

Riall led a second expedition across the river, capturing the gun position at Lewiston and setting fire to the village "to deprive the enemy of cover for his troops." Both Fort George and Fort Niagara were occupied and improved while Riall and his men destroyed the villages of Black Rock and Buffalo, acquiring yet more booty. Apparently satisfied that enough had been done to revenge the burning of Newark, or fearful of future retaliation, Drummond ordered his troops to cease pursuing this "system of warfare, so revolting to his own feelings and so little congenial to the British character."

Operations in the Northwest, 1813

After the battle of the River Raisin, 22 January 1813, Harrison gave up his plans for a winter campaign to recapture Detroit and Fort Malden withdrawing to a secure position south of the Maumee Rapids. Much of the militia was determined to go home, their six month term of service ended. Harrison arranged to build a large fort above the rapids, naming it Fort Meigs after the Governor of Ohio. He then left for Cincinnati to raise new militia units from Kentucky, Indiana, and Ohio. Harrison was convinced he needed at least 10,000 men under arms to garrison the frontier posts and prepare for a summer invasion of Canada. The Secretary of War, John Armstrong, insisted that the campaign could only take place after the U.S. Navy had won control of Lake Erie and he outlined the steps the government had taken to assemble a powerful fleet at Presque Ile (Erie), Pennsylvania.

The naval race on Lake Erie began in earnest when Master Commandant Oliver Hazard Perry arrived at Presque Ile in the spring of 1813. Two 20-gun brigs, *Niagara* and *Lawrence*, were under construction and once equipped and launched, control of the lake might well pass to the Americans. Perry was able to take advantage of a relatively favourable logistical situation. Much of the equipment to outfit the ships could be obtained in Pittsburgh, a town of 9,000 people with iron forges and cordage works, or Philadelphia, the port city connected to Pittsburgh by what passed for good roads.

The contrast between American and Canadian logistics was striking. Virtually everything needed in ship construction except the wood had to come from England then make its way by steamboat from Québec City to Montréal for transfer to battle which took on average eight days to reach Kingston. From there, providing the Americans did not control Lake Ontario, supplies for Amherstburg would arrive at Fort George in two to three days, be offloaded, moved around Niagara Falls, and finally by sail to Amherstburg.

During the winter of 1812-13, the urgency of the naval race on Lake Erie led the British to ship naval stores overland to Fort York and when the Americans attacked, the supplies intended for Amherstburg – "cables, cordage, canvas, tools, and stores of every kind" – were burned to prevent them from falling into enemy hands. Commodore Chauncey regarded this as the real significance of the victory at Fort York. The British commander had "received a blow," he wrote, "from which he cannot recover."

At Amherstburg the *Detroit*, Barclay's flagship, could only be completed with improvised fittings and cannons of various calibres borrowed from the walls of Fort Malden. The American advantage in logistics and their temporary success at York and Fort George tipped the scales on Lake Erie.

The First Siege of Fort Meigs, 1813

The British government and its representative in Canada, Sir George Prévost, was kept fully informed of the American decision to commit both money and manpower to the recovery of the Northwest and the defeat of the First Nations. This new strategy ought to have forced the British to reconsider the contradiction in their own strategy but events in North America were still of secondary importance. The original policy based on protecting Montréal and Québec even at the sacrifice of Upper Canada had been compromised by pledges of support

William H. Harrison. [R. Peale]

for some kind of First Nations "buffer state" south of the lakes. No one seemed to know how this might be achieved without control of the lakes, massive reinforcements, and a protracted war.

Strategic confusion results in operational uncertainty as events in the Northwest in 1813 were to demonstrate. The newly promoted Brigadier-General Henry Proctor had withdrawn his forces after the battle at the River Raisin, deciding against pursuing Harrison's demoralized army. When Harrison began to build Fort Meigs, Roundhead, the First Nation's spokesman in Tecumseh's absence, urged an immediate attack but Prévost was opposed and Proctor, concerned about further losses to his small regular army decided to wait for the end of winter, the return of Tecumseh and the arrival of reinforcements. The capture of York cancelled the westward move of the promised companies of the 41st Regiment, leaving Proctor with little choice except to rely on his own resources, 533 regulars and 462 militia. The large and growing body of First Nations warriors, perhaps 3,000 men, was of limited value in a siege against a heavily fortified position like Fort Meigs but they had to be fed and supplied with ammunition straining an already precarious logistical situation.

Proctor began the siege of Fort Meigs on 27 April, but his light guns were unable to breach the forts wooden walls and the Americans dug 12 foot high earthen mounds and traverses within the perimeter as an effective protection from cannon balls. Harrison ignored Tecumseh's challenge to stop hiding in the earth "like a ground hog" and waited for a relief column of Kentucky volunteers to arrive. On 5 May, day eight of the siege, the Kentucky Militia arrived. One regiment attempted to seize the British batteries across from the fort. Shouting "Remember the Raisin," they charged and soon lost all cohesion. Over 500 were encircled and surrendered. Again accounts of what followed vary widely but a number of American prisoners were killed before the combined efforts of Tecumseh and the Indian agents ended the bloodshed.

Tecumseh saving American prisoners from the slaughter. [LC USZ62-46488]

The surrender of yet more Kentucky Militia allowed Proctor to claim a tactical victory but Fort Meigs had been reinforced and resupplied. A new set of horror stories about massacres and British complicity were in circulation throughout the United States, encouraging enlistment and further talk of revenge. Operationally, the British and First Nations situation deteriorated. The siege of Fort Meigs demonstrated that Proctors' small army lacked the capacity to capture a fortified position raising serious doubts among First Nations leaders about the value of the alliance. Growing tension between the allies was compounded by the supply problem. Feeding and providing ammunition to large numbers of warriors was a logistical nightmare for Proctor, particularly after a new, large party of warriors arrived from the upper Great Lakes.

The contrast between the uncertain situation facing Proctor and the systematic American preparations at Fort Meigs and the naval base at Presque Ile was striking. The shorter supply lines and proximity to the settled areas of Ohio and Pennsylvania allowed Harrison to feed, equip, and train a new army while Perry completed construction of a fleet capable of challenging British control of Lake Erie. Once it became clear the limited forces at Amherstburg would not be reinforced the obvious course of action – an attack on Presque Ile – was ruled out. Instead he agreed to a plan, apparently proposed by Tecumseh, to lure the Americans at Fort Meigs into open battle.

Tecumseh's idea was to simulate a battle with an imaginary column of American reinforcements, persuading the garrison to leave the safety of the fort. This plan failed when the Americans stayed within the fort's walls. Proctor abandoned Fort Meigs and moved his regulars to the Sandusky River to attack Fort Stephenson, a small, isolated post defended by 160 men led by a determined commander, Major George Croghan. The 41st Regiment attacked with great courage but were repulsed with heavy losses. The First Nations warriors watched this failed attack with dismay, their dreams of checking American expansion with British help shattered.

The defeat and surrender of the British naval squadron on Lake Erie, 10 September 1813, ended any remaining hope of maintaining British control of Michigan and Southwestern Upper Canada. The American fleet, commanded by Oliver Perry, included two new 20-gun brigs, *Niagara* and *Lawrence*, and four smaller vessels built at Presque Ile, plus the three that had escaped from Black Rock. Robert Barclay, who had taken command of the six British ships at Amherstburg, was short of trained men and much else. His flagship, the newly built *Detroit*, had been hastily equipped with a variety of guns and was most effective at long range. Perry was determined to force a close action where the much greater weight of fire of his guns would be decisive. Both *Niagara* and *Lawrence* mounted 36, 32-pounder carronades which would be devastating at close range.

The Battle of Lake Erie, also known as the Battle of Put-in-Bay. This 1911 painting illustrates Perry moving from the *Lawrence* to the *Niagara*. [Percy Moran, LC-USZC4-6893]

The desperate supply situation at Amherstburg led Barclay to leave his protected anchorage on 9 September. Perry's squadron sailed from Put-in-Bay to meet the British line. The wind was briefly in Barclay's favour, permitting him to begin the action at long range, but when the wind shifted Perry closed the gap. An intense, brutal exchange of broadsides so damaged *Lawrence* that Perry shifted his flag to *Niagara* before renewing the battle. With every British officer wounded or dead Barclay surrendered and Perry sent his famous signal: "We have met the enemy and they are ours."

When news of Barclay's defeat reached Proctor he decided to abandon Detroit and Fort Malden, withdrawing along the River Thames to Burlington. Tecumseh protested calling Proctor a coward but the British general was no longer willing to consider the views of First Nations leaders. Proctor had agreed to Tecumseh's attack on Fort Meigs and the attempt to capture Fort Stephenson. On both occasions the warriors had largely stood by, waiting for the British to breach the fortress walls. The logistics of feeding and supplying thousands of warriors and their families gathered at Amherstburg, combined with uncertainty about their willingness to resist the large American army moving relentlessly north, persuaded Proctor that retreat was inevitable.

The disaster that overwhelmed Proctor at the Battle of the Thames has called his decision into question. Would it not have been better to employ his forces, close to 1,000 regulars and a large contingent of warriors in organized battle against Harrison and his Kentucky and Ohio Militia? The most damning criticism of Proctor is his conduct of the retreat which was delayed, slow, and disorganized.

Harrison's army was augmented by a force of mounted Kentucky volunteers commanded by Colonel Richard Johnson. With a strength of more than 1,000 men, they shared a determination to revenge the heavy losses suffered

"Remember the River Raisin!" [Ken Riley, National Guard]

by Kentuckians at the River Raisin and Fort Meigs. Johnson's regiment was a formidable striking force. The rest of Harrison's army crossed Lake Erie on the surviving vessels of Perry's squadron and followed the Kentucky volunteers along the River Thames.

The British withdrawal began on 22 September when women, children, the sick, and prisoners were moved by boats to Chatham. Two days later the main force followed. Most of the warriors left for their homelands, but Tecumseh with 700 men agreed to join Proctor on the understanding that the British would make a firm stand at Chatham which was to be fortified.

There are conflicting accounts of the British failure to burn the bridges behind them and various versions of the reasons for their slow progress including bad roads and heavy rain. The result is not in dispute. Despite a six day head start, Johnson's cavalry quickly caught up with Proctor and Tecumseh who turned to give battle near the Moravian mission-village of Fairfield (Moraviantown). The regulars formed a line in a lightly-wooded area between the river and a marsh. Tecumseh's warriors occupied a separate position in a swamp where they hoped to attack the American flank. Proctor formed a reserve line 200 yards to the rear, diminishing the fire power of the normal tactical formation. The battle began when half of Johnson's cavalry charged the front line which broke and retreated in disorder. Less than twenty minutes later the British regulars threw down their arms and surrendered. Proctor and his staff escaped west.

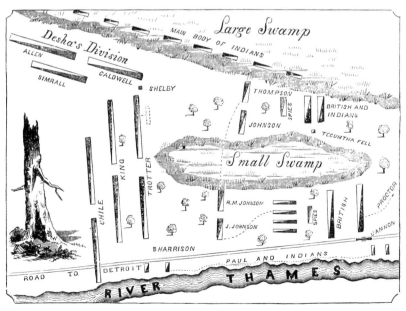

This sketch detailing the battle was designed for Benten Henderson Young's 1903 publication *The Battle of The Thames*. Though we know the battle took place near Moriavantown and along the River Thames, historians have been unable to identify the exact location.

Colonel Johnson personally led the attack on the warriors and is usually credited with killing Tecumseh though he himself was wounded in the first charge. The warriors, perhaps 500 strong at the beginning of the battle, melted away into the wilderness. Some of Harrison's men looted and burned the village of Fairfield, adding to the list of atrocities committed by both sides.

The American victory at the battle of the Thames ended the war on the Michigan-Ohio frontier but Michlimackinac and the areas on either side of the Upper Great Lakes remained under British and First Nations control. The war in the Northwest was not yet over.

Death of Tecumseh: Battle of the Thames Oct. 18 1813. [LC USZC4-1581]

The Creek Wars

The transformation of the War of 1812 from a struggle over impressment and neutral rights at sea into a war against the First Nations on the American frontier was evident in the campaign to destroy the militant warriors of the Creek nation known as "Red Sticks." By 1813, the Creeks were broadly divided into two factions. The southern villages near the Chattahoochee River in Alabama had come to terms with the United States, but the villages in northern Alabama remained hostile particularly when confronted with demands to allow roads to be constructed through their territory.

The Creeks were also caught up in the American scheme to win control of East Florida from Spain. West Florida, the panhandle, was claimed by the United States as part of the Louisiana Purchase and occupied in 1810 but there were no reasonable grounds for seizing the Florida peninsula unless the Spanish could be linked to First Nations resistance. Open hostilities began on 27 July 1813 when American settlers attacked a band of Creeks returning from Florida with arms and ammunition supplied by the Spanish at Pensacola. Known as the Battle of Burnt Corn Creek, this clash started a new conflict that led to open civil war among the Creeks when the southern villages sided with the United States.

Massacre at Fort Mims, 30 August 1813. [Tennessee Historical Society]

On 30 August 1813 the Creek Red Sticks attacked Fort Mims, the major American bastion in Alabama, killing most of the garrison and the civilians who had taken refuge. The massacre prompted Tennessee to authorize Andrew Jackson to lead a punitive expedition to overwhelm the Red Sticks. Finally in March 1814, Jackson's army won a battle at the Horseshoe Bend of the Tallapoosa River. The massacre that followed forced the surviving Red Sticks to flee to Spanish Florida where, together with native Seminoles and escaped slaves, they survived until Jackson's invasion of Florida in 1818.

Depiction of William Weatherford surrendering to Andrew Jackson after the Battle of Horseshoe Bend. Jackson was so impressed with Weatherford's disposition he set him free. [LC DIG-ppmsca-32639]

Montréal

Throughout the summer of 1813, Prévost continued to hold most of the British regulars in Lower Canada despite evidence that the American forces in the Champlain Valley were far from ready to carry out an offensive against Montréal. In early July two American warships, the sloops *Growler* and *Eagle* sailed too far up the Richelieu and were captured at Île-aux-Noix. Renamed the *Brooke* and *Shannon*, they added to a British fleet which easily dominated Lake Champlain.

The temptation to use naval superiority proved too much for Prévost who authorized Lieutenant-Colonel John Murray and naval Lieutenant Daniel Pring to sweep the lake clear of American ships and destroy all public buildings, military stores, and vessels within reach. As a joint military operation, what became known as "Murray's Raid," 14 July - 3 August, was a grand success. In strategic terms it was a disaster for it persuaded the Americans to create a new, secure naval yard at Vergennes, Vermont and begin a construction program to regain control of their territorial waters.

Murray's Raid also focused attention on the scattered elements of Major-General Wade Hampton's command in Vermont and northern New York. Hampton, a wealthy South Carolinian planter, had been a Revolutionary War hero but at 62 years of age he was a strange choice, totally unsuited to an active command of a northern theatre of war. Over the summer a number of new regular army regiments arrived at Burlington and Plattsburgh, but they were regulars in name only. Largely untrained and ill-disciplined, the 1,000 men supported by 1,500 militia did not seem like an offensive force able to march on Montréal.

After the battle of Beaver Dams, 24 June 1813, the U.S. Secretary of War, John Armstrong, dismissed General Dearborn replacing him with another revolutionary war veteran, Major-General James Wilkinson. A

James Wilkinson. [Charles W. Peale]   Wade Hampton. [NYPL 421378]

major reason for selecting Wilkinson was to replace him in command of New Orleans as he was thought to be too incompetent and corrupt to serve there. Armstrong knew that Wilkinson and Hampton were bitter enemies so he agreed to allow Hampton to receive his orders directly from the War Department, not through Wilkinson. These complications made coordinating offensive operations very difficult but by the end of August Wilkinson had won Armstrong's approval for a plan "to make a bold feint at Kingston slip down the St. Lawrence and in concert with the division under General Hampton take Montréal." Wilkinson failed to explain how a feint in the direction of Kingston could be sustained after an army of 8,000 men on 300 boats had moved downriver from Sackets Harbor towards Montréal, leaving a substantial enemy army at Kingston able to follow and harass them.

While Wilkinson waited for his armada to be readied, Hampton began concentrating his army north of Plattsburgh on 20 September. After crossing the border at Odelltown he decided that a prolonged drought in the area south of Montréal required the army to advance down the Châteauguay River. On 26 September the troops marched to Four Corners, the present day location of Chateauguay, New York.

The challenge of coordinating the actions of the two armies now became crucial. Armstrong urged Hampton not to move from Four Corners until Wilkinson's army approached Montréal. "We ought," he wrote, "run no risks by separate attacks when combined ones are practicable and sure." Despite this plea Hampton began his advance into Canada on 21 October before learning that Wilkinson's flotilla had run into an autumn storm and were regrouping at Grenadier Island, a mere 12 miles from Sackets Harbor.

Hampton's army of some 4,000 men included 1,500 New York Militia who refused to cross the border but the force advancing down the Châteauguay River included 2,000 infantry, 200 cavalry, and ten field guns. Major-General Louis de Watteville, a Swiss professional soldier who was responsible for the defence of Montréal, commanded roughly 8,000 militia as well as several thousand regular soldiers including Meuron's Swiss Regiment, the Canadian Fencibles, the Glengarry Fencibles, and the Voltigeurs Canadiens. The Voltigeurs were led by a British professional soldier from Lower Canada, Charles-Michel

1924 Molson Advertisement featuring Charles de Salaberry. [LAC C-009226]

A painting of the Canadian Voltigeurs near Lacolle in 1812. [Parks Canada]

D'Irumberry de Salaberry. De Watteville had ample time to prepare defences to block the American advance as Hampton took four days to advance 23 miles to present-day Ormstown. A series of small creeks enter the river below Ormstown and each became a blocking position with barriers made of fallen trees known as abitis. de Salaberry and his men occupied the forward line near Allan's Corners and prepared to meet the Americans.

On 25 October, Hampton split his force sending a column under Colonel Robert Purdy across to the south bank of the river with orders to bypass the Voltigeurs and ford the river as one arm of a pincer attack. Purdy's men attempted a night march over eight miles of trackless woods and swamps and were consequently in poor shape when confronted with concentrated fire from a company posted on the south bank. Brigadier George Izard, who commanded the main American column, thought that the sounds of battle meant Purdy's men were across the river and attacking from the rear. He ordered his troops forward where they were met by disciplined fire from the Voltigeurs. Both Purdy and Izard were to claim that the attack could have been successfully pressed if Hampton had not ordered a withdrawal, but given the presence of Lieutenant-Colonel George Macdonell's Glengarry Fencibles in close reserve and more Canadians available in the immediate vicinity, Hampton made a wise decision. His army returned to Four Corners on 28 October and he informed Wilkinson that there would be no further advance on Montréal from the south. Hampton had been ordered to prepare winter quarters for his troops before the action on the Châteauguay River, suggesting that the Americans had no intention of reaching Montréal if any serious opposition was met.

Despite the news of Hampton's withdrawal, Wilkinson ordered his army to resume the advance requesting Hampton to join him at St. Régis. The

The Battle of Crysler's Farm, 1813

flotilla finally got underway again on 5 November, passing Fort Wellington and reaching Ogdensburg. The weather was miserable, as was normal for November. Wilkinson called for a war council inviting his senior officers to offer opinions about a further advance on Montréal. Given the lateness of the season, the presence of a force of British regulars and a squadron of British gunboats nipping at his heels, the uncertainty about Hampton's intentions, and the losses of arms, rations, and boats in the autumn storm, sensible men would have immediately abandoned the expedition. Instead, everyone agreed that there was no honourable alternative except to go on. Before running the rapids at the Long Sault General Brown wanted to clear the enemy holding the riverbank at Cornwall. He ordered Colonel Alexander McComb to land his reserve brigade, about 1,200 men on the northern shore near Morristown. They put a scratch force of Canadians to flight, seized an unmanned, incomplete fort at Matilda (Iroquois), and continued east where they were joined by 500 dragoons under General Jacob Brown. He divided his troops ordering General John Parker Boyd to form a rear guard providing protection from the British who had been reinforced with troops from Fort Wellington. They now totalled more than 800 men.

Lieutenant-Colonel Joseph Morrison of the 89th Regiment led this corps d'observation with Lieutenant-Colonel John Harvey, the hero of Stoney Creek, as his second-in-command. Commander William Mulcaster of the Royal Navy added experience in the use of the gunboats and it was Mulcaster who began the action of 11 November 1813, opening fire on the American boats at Crysler's Island. Morrison's skirmishers began to attack, forcing the Americans to turn and fight. General Boyd organized his men into three columns and moved off towards Crysler's Farm. It was raining and the fields were muddy, American morale was low and supplies of ammunition limited. After four hours of attack and counter-attack Boyd withdrew leaving

A detail of the battle at *Crysler's Farm*. [Adam Sheriff Scott]

History

Morrison in control of the battlefield. Losses were heavy – 439 American casualties and 179 British – but nothing had been settled. If Wilkinson continued the advance Morrison would have had to follow and force a second encounter. After yet another war council and the arrival of the letter from Hampton declining to move his men to St. Régis, the Americans voted to abandon the advance and withdraw across the border to find winter quarters for the army at French Mills, renamed Fort Covington. The usual pattern of sickness and death marked the winter in northern New York.

This First World War Propaganda Poster evokes 1812 and de Salaberry's brave French troops. [LC-USZC4-12727]

The Rival Strategies, 1814

For the United States of America, the year 1813 ended in a series of tactical defeats at Châteauguay, Crysler's Farm, and Fort Niagara. The destruction of Napoleon's army at the Battle of Leipzig in October 1813 pointed to an even greater threat to American ambitions as the British would soon be able to transfer troops to North America. On 10 January 1814, President Madison accepted a British offer to begin direct negotiations to end the war. This decision, which implied the abandonment of dreams of conquering Canada, was bitterly opposed by the Secretary of War, John Armstrong, and frontier state politicians who were determined to consolidate their western victories, removing the threat of British support for the First Nations. Madison fended off his critics by appointing Henry Clay, the leading "Warhawk," as one of the peace negotiators, persuading critics that Clay would never sacrifice western interests.

Congress accepted the necessity of continuing the war until a satisfactory peace agreement was reached but once again refused to agree on tax measures to finance the war effort. This left Madison with few options and it was not until June 1814 that a limited campaign in the Niagara region and an expedition to recover Michlimackinac were authorized. Neither of these ventures seriously threatened British power in North America, suggesting how limited American offensive capacity was in 1814.

British strategy was far more ambitious. Despite the advice of the Duke of Wellington, who argued that no military operation Britain had the capacity to carry out would do sufficient injury to the United States to force them to sue for peace, new offensive operations were authorized. The protection of Canada was still the primary objective but with 10,000 additional troops on their way to the St. Lawrence, plans for occupying northern Maine, recovering Amherstburg, and seizing control of Plattsburgh and the western shore of Lake Champlain were developed. Admiral Alexander Cochrane, who had extended his blockade of the middle atlantic and southern ports to New England in April 1814, was given the resources to mount operations against Washington and preparations to close the mouth of the Mississippi and capture New Orleans were begun. The British government did not plan to conquer the United States. Their intent was to seek revenge and humiliate a country that had joined their enemies at a crucial moment in the war against Napoleon.

History

The Battle of Chippawa, 1814

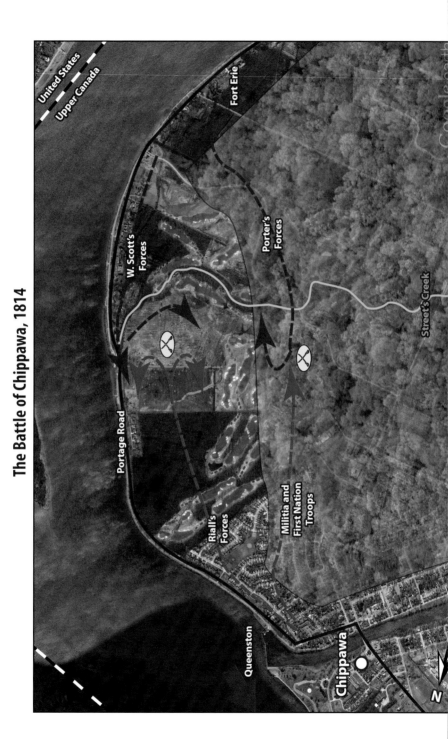

American Operations, 1814

The regular army of the United States of America numbered 23,000 at the beginning of 1814 but the terms of enlistment of more than half of these men were due to expire during the year. This situation meant that on the Canadian front only one relatively small American army could attempt offensive operations in 1814. General Jacob Brown commanded this force, which was responsible for the defence of Sackets Harbor as well as a projected offensive in the Niagara.

The units training at Buffalo included Brigadier-General Winfield Scott's 1st Brigade, numbering 1,400 men. The 2nd Brigade, Brigadier General Eleazar Ripley, was smaller with just over 1,000 "present for duty." Militia from New York and Pennsylvania under Brigadier Peter Porter, together with a large, 500 warrior group from the Six Nations led by Red Jacket, the Seneca Chief, raised the total strength available to General Brown to just under 5,000 men.

The American commanders were divided by personal quarrels and genuine differences over the purpose and scope of the campaign. Brown's plan called for the two regular army brigades to cross the Niagara River, cut off and occupy Fort Erie, then advance along the river to attack Fort George. If Chauncey's Lake Ontario fleet supported further action, Fort Niagara might be recovered and an advance to Burlington Heights carried out. Scott was anxious to test his well-trained brigade against the British regulars but Ripley objected to every aspect of the plan. He wanted to know where supplies of food, ammunition, and replacements for the inevitable casualties would come from. How would the problems of the 1813 campaign be overcome? What was the point, he asked, to fighting merely for the sake of fighting? Ripley's proffered resignation was refused and he reluctantly led his brigade into Canada.

The small British garrison at Fort Erie surrendered on 3 July and Brown ordered the advance to continue. Riall gathered his forces at Chippawa using First Nations warriors and militias to harass and slow the American advance. Scott's brigade reached Streets Creek on the evening of 4 July, pausing to prepare an organized attack across the Chippawa River. The next day, Porter's militia and some 400 warriors began to clear the wooded flank. Upon reaching the Chippawa, Porter discovered that the British had crossed the river and were preparing to attack what General Riall believed was a small contingent of "Buffalo militia." Porter's men fled, pursued by John Norton's Grand River warriors.

The Americans reacted swiftly to news of the British advance. Scott's brigade was preparing for a delayed 4th of July parade and was ready to move. Ripley's brigade was ordered to join them as soon as possible. Riall's decision

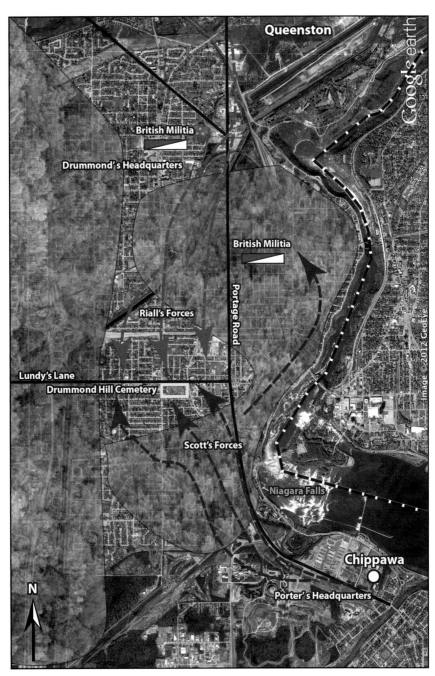

The Battle of Lundy's Lane, 1814

to abandon a strong defensive position behind a fast flowing river and advance over open ground towards the American lines has been attributed to poor intelligence as well as arrogance and stupidity. The forces engaged at Chippawa were roughly equal in strength but this time the Americans prevailed. Historian George Stanley described the tactics employed in the battle: "Load and fire; advance a few paces; halt, load, and fire again… As the British advanced, Winfield Scott held back his centre, pushing forward his wings, thus exposing the attacking force to both frontal and flank fire." The casualties in this encounter were dreadful. Scott's brigade had 41 killed and 221 wounded. The British losses – 145 killed, 321 wounded, and 46 missing – added up to a third of all those engaged.

The Americans advancing at Chippawa. [H. Charles McBarron Jr.]

After Chippawa, the British withdrew to Fort George and Burlington. The Americans regrouped and waited for Chauncey's fleet to bring heavy guns, supplies, and reinforcements for a replay of the 1813 campaign. It was not to be. Chauncey had no intention of risking his fleet to support Brown's quixotic venture. General Brown now faced a difficult situation. Reinforcements, regulars, fencibles, and militia were joining the British forces, threatening an advance on the American side of the river from Fort Niagara to Buffalo or a flanking attack designed to envelope and destroy their army in Canada. Brown decided to renew the attempt to capture Fort George, ordering Winfield Scott's 1st Brigade to lead the advance. When the Americans reached the rising ground at Lundy's Lane on 25 July, they encountered a substantial British force. Riall gave orders to withdraw but these were countermanded by Drummond.

History

Both Drummond and Scott were determined to fight and Drummond quickly organized his forces to take advantage of the terrain, placing his artillery and a battery of congreve rockets at the top of the hill near the church. Scott sent a message to Brown urging him to send the other brigades forward but he did not wait for their arrival and instead launched a series of costly frontal attacks. One American battalion used the cover of the woods to cross Lundy's Lane and get behind the British position. They captured a number of prisoners including General Riall but then withdrew.

As darkness fell, Ripley's brigade renewed the battle, gaining the hill and seizing the British guns. British and Canadian accounts of the battle, relying on Drummond's dispatch describe a series of ultimately successful counterattacks. The American version portrays a tactical victory defending the hill "with bayonets and clubbed muskets… in darkness made more impenetrable by the heavy pall of smoke." With Scott's brigade shattered and their aggressive General seriously wounded, Brown, who was himself suffering from a painful wound, ordered Ripley, now the senior surviving officer, to withdraw to Chippawa and take the captured guns with him. The Americans desperately needed "food, ammunition, and above all, water," but once re-organized Brown wanted Ripley to renew the attack

Ripley appears to have been the only commanding officer on either side who understood that the purpose of battle was to achieve operational effects that advanced strategic interests. He had opposed Brown's summer offensive because the army lacked the manpower and logistical strength to achieve

The Battle of Lundy's Lane. [C.W. Jeffreys]

significant results. On the morning of 26 July he knew that his men had not been able to remove or destroy the British guns and the hill was once again manned by British regulars. Ripley refused to renew the action and destroyed the bridge over the Chippawa, ordering the army to withdraw to Fort Erie. Ripley then sought Brown's permission to bring the army back to Buffalo, ending the campaign. When Brown refused Ripley demanded a written order for what he saw as a pointless exercise. Order in hand, Ripley began the task of re-building the defences of Fort Erie, America's last toehold on Canadian territory.

Lundy's Lane cost the Americans 171 killed, 572 wounded, and 110 missing. The British reported 84 killed and 559 wounded with 169 taken prisoner. Roughly one third of all those who fought at Lundy's Lane became casualties or prisoners of war. Drummond was among the British wounded and this, together with the heavy losses, may account for his reluctance to follow up the American withdrawal. By 1 August he had received substantial reinforcements and begun preparations to force the enemy to abandon Fort Erie. Drummond sent 600 men across the river "to destroy the enemy's supply depots at Black Rock and Buffalo." If this action had succeeded, the garrison in Fort Erie "would have been compelled by want of provisions to come out and fight or surrender" but the British found the bridge over the Scajaquada Creek destroyed and a battalion of American infantry posted on the far bank. An attempt to rush the bridge failed as did a manoeuvre to outflank the defences.

The American perspective at Lundy's Lane. [Alonzo Chappel, LC USZ62-48155]

Drummond decided to prepare a systematic siege of the Fort relying on heavy guns to breach the fortress walls before launching an attack. Colonel Hercules Scott, who had joined Drummond's army at Lundy's Lane, observed the preparations for the assault and, fearing the result, wrote to his brother to settle his affairs. Scott was not impressed with Drummond's leadership qualities and he found the preparations for the assault 'inadequate.' "I have little hope of success from this maneuver," he wrote prophetically.

On 14 August, Drummond, who apparently believed that the bombardment begun the day before had made a "sufficient impression... on the works of the enemy's fort," ordered an assault on Fort Erie. His decision may have been influenced by the ease with which a small party of 70 seamen and marines captured two of the three American schooners positioned to provide flank protection to the Fort. Drummond devised an elaborate plan for a night attack that called for close coordination of three columns of troops. The most challenging task fell to Lieutenant-Colonel Victor Fischer who led a force of some 1,300 men on a circuitous six-hour march through forest and swamp to attack Snake Hill, a fortified position on the American left flank. Drummond had insisted that to ensure surprise, all but "a reserve of select and steady men were to remove the flints from their flintlocks" to avoid an accidental discharge.

Despite a determined attempt to outflank the American defences by wading chest-high into the water and a brave attempt to rush the main position with scaling ladders that proved too short, Fischer's men were repulsed with heavy losses. The other two columns also attacked and the left-hand column lost 30% of its men, including Hercules Scott. On their third attempt, the centre companies gained control of the northeast bastion and for a brief moment could imagine achieving victory until a massive explosion of the powder magazine sent "fragments of timber, stone, and bodies of men... one or two hundred feet in the air." The explosion killed or wounded 400 men and shattered British morale and the ill-conceived attack ended.

Major-General Edmund Gaines, Resolution of Congress Medal for the Battle of Erie. [Lossing]

Drummond was unwilling to abandon the siege which continued even after a successful American sortie on 17 September overran two British gun batteries, bringing the total casualties in one of the bloodiest battles ever to take place on Canadian soil to 1,500 British and roughly 700 Americans. Drummond finally conceded defeat and withdrew to Chippawa.

The utter confusion that characterized American strategic direction of the war once again loomed large. In one of his final directives issued just before the burning of Washington ended his career, Secretary of War John Armstrong ordered Major-General George Izard to move a large part of the army's defending the Lake Champlain invasion route to Sackets Harbor for an attack on Kingston. Izard protested, arguing that the build-up of British troops in Lower Canada indicated an early offensive against Plattsburgh, but Armstrong insisted on the move. When Izard's army reached Sackets Harbor, he discovered that the navy would not cooperate so he decided on his own to respond to a request to join a new attempt to win control of the forts on the Niagara.

Izard's 4,000 men reached Lewiston in early October with plans to attack the British garrison at Fort Niagara. After a brief reconnaissance it was evident that without heavy guns the Fort was impregnable so Izard crossed the river to mount a new offensive against the British at Chippawa. An encounter battle between an American brigade and a British force at Lyon's Creek, fought in a cold October rain, was a tactical victory for the Glengarries and British regulars that served to discourage further attacks. Izard concluded that continuing the campaign made little sense. He made plans to destroy Fort Erie and retire to the American side of the river. On 5 November 1814, the Fort was rocked with explosions and the last American soldiers left the Niagara.

The Ruins of Fort Erie, 1860. [Lossing]

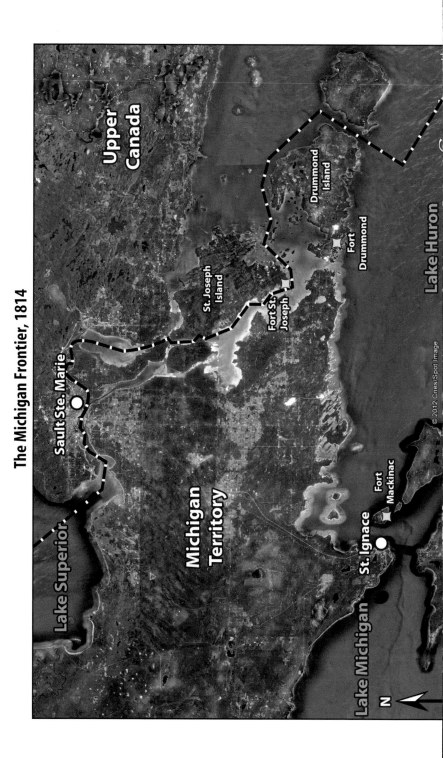

The Michigan Frontier, 1814

The War in the West, 1814

The American victory at Moraviantown, the Battle of the Thames, in October 1813 did not end the war in the west nor the dream of a separate First Nations territory. The First Nations of the western Great Lakes/Upper Mississippi region were still autonomous, linked with British Indian agents and Canadian fur traders at Prairie du Chien, Green Bay, and Michilimackinac. Late in the spring of 1814 William Clark, the Governor of Missouri Territory, sent an expedition up the Mississippi to establish American authority at Prairie du Chien. A number of gunboats, the largest capable of carrying 100 men plus the oarsmen, sailed and rowed up river with their cannons and swivel guns, overrowing the Saux and Fox warriors who watched from the riverbanks. Clark's men established a stockade and blockhouse at Prairie du Chien, naming it Fort Shelby. A garrison of 70 men and a gunboat were left to defend this new post while the rest of the expedition returned to St. Louis in triumph.

The newly appointed British commander of Fort Michilimackinac, Lieutenant-Colonel Robert McDouall, was working hard to strengthen the defences of Mackinac Island. By building an additional fort on the high ground he hoped to prevent the Americans from using the approach the British had taken when capturing the island in 1812. Despite good intelligence on American plans to attack his post, McDouall organized an expedition to recover Prairie du Chien. In a letter sent to Sir Gordon Drummond after the force left for the Mississippi, McDouall wrote that it was necessary "to dislodge the American General from his new conquest. Prairie du Chien must be recovered or our connection with the Indians would be destroyed, as would the only barrier which protects the great trading establishments of the North West and the Hudson's Bay Companies."

McDouall gathered a force of local residents enlisted as Michigan Fencibles, a Royal Artillery gunner with an easily portable three-pounder gun and more than 100 warriors. William McKay, an experienced fur trader, was made a temporary Lieutenant-Colonel and he, along with Major Toussaint Pothier's voyageurs, led the party south. At Green Bay, local settlers and a growing band of warriors, Sioux, Winnebagos, Foxes, Sacs, and Kickapoos joined the expedition. They reached Prairie du Chien on 17 July and used the canon to force the gunboat to withdraw downriver. Fort Shelby surrendered when the garrison was threatened by the prospect of red-hot cannon balls. McKay promised to protect the paroled militia who began the 600 mile journey downriver to St. Louis. They met an American relief column which had been mauled by warriors of the Saux, Fox, and Kickapoo nations. Both groups withdrew to the south.

History

Watercolour depicting the American surrender at Fort Shelby, Prairie du Chien. [Seth Eastman]

Governor Clark appointed Major Zachary Taylor, who would later use his military career as a credential to win the presidential election of 1848, to restore the situation at Prairie du Chien. With some 350 regular troops and eight gunboats, the new expedition encountered more than 1,000 warriors under the charismatic leadership of Black Hawk, the Saux chief. Supported by a contingent of Royal Artillery with two swivel guns and the three-pounder, the warriors attacked Taylor's flotilla, forcing the Americans to retreat. Prairie du Chien and the Northwest remained free of American influence until March 1815 when news of the peace treaty reached the area. The British post, Fort McKay, was burned and the garrison withdrew to

The British three-Pounder. The weapon was essential for laying siege on forts. [Department of National Defence]

Mackinac and then St. Joseph's Island, leaving the First Nations to the tender mercies of the "long knives."

The American attempt to recover Mackinac Island began as an ambitious plan to control Lake Huron, seizing the British supply bases established at Matchedash and Nottawasaga before sailing north to assault the main British stronghold on the upper lakes. A large fleet including the *Niagara* and the other surviving ships from the Battle of Lake Erie failed to locate the supply depots on Georgian Bay but destroyed a hastily abandoned post on St. Joseph's Island. At Mackinac Island, Colonel George Croghan, the hero of the Battle of Fort Stephenson, found that the fleet's guns could not be elevated enough to strike either fort. He decided to land his forces and undertake a deliberate advance, luring the garrison and the warriors into open field combat.

McDouall, concerned that his First Nations allies would leave the island if he simply defended his forts, gave battle with a contingent of Royal Newfoundland Fencibles, local militia, and Royal Artillery gunners flanked by several hundred warriors, Winnebagos, Chippawas, and Ottawas. The Americans faced a well-organized defensive position forcing them to advance across open fields to reach the edge of the forest. Accounts of the battle that followed present a confused picture of warrior attacks, a frontal assault, tactical withdrawals, and ultimately the decision to abandon the

Two Ottawa Chiefs who with others lately came down from Michilimackinac, Lake Huron to have a talk with their great father the King and his representative. [LAC-C-114384]

battlefield when Croghan determined that success was unlikely and "there was no sense in further exposing his men to British fire." American losses – 13 killed, 46 wounded, and two missing – were enough to discourage any further attempts to return to the island which the British held until the end of the war. Most of the American ships and militia returned to Detroit but Croghan, with three ships, sailed to the Nottawasaga River hoping to destroy the schooner *Nancy* that was being used to supply Michilimackinac. Forewarned, the captain of the *Nancy* had moved the vessel up river where a recently-built blockhouse offered some protection. Croghan landed an assault force with howitzers and began to fire on the blockhouse. Croghan's account of the battle claimed that accurate howitzer fire forced a British retreat, exploded the magazine, and set fire to the *Nancy*. Lieutenant Miller Worsley, Royal Navy, reported that he had given the order to explode the magazine, withdrawing the small garrison in good order. In both versions the *Nancy* was destroyed and the supplies at Nottawasaga looted. Croghan returned to Detroit leaving two small schooners, *Tigress* and *Scorpion*, to intercept British vessels on Lake Huron.

Lieutenant Worsley and his men brought their wounded with them on a thirty-six mile trek to a store house at Penetanguishene. From there Worsley and eighteen seamen sailed two open boats to Michlimackinac 380 miles, bypassing the American warships and blockading the island during the night.

The Schooner *Nancy*. [Seth Eastman]

Worsley was then joined by Lieutenant Andrew Bulger and his men from the Royal Newfoundland Fencibles in a cutting out expedition that captured the *Tigress*. The next night, the *Scorpion*, returning from a patrol, anchored close by and a boarding party seized the schooner after overcoming "sharp resistance." In a letter to his father, Worsley reported that "after a series of hardships I have got two schooners both finer vessels than the *Nancy*..." He had also won command of the waters of Lake Huron for the balance of the war.

Studio portrait taken in July 1882 of the surviving Six Nations warriors who fought with the British in the War of 1812. [LAC C-085127]

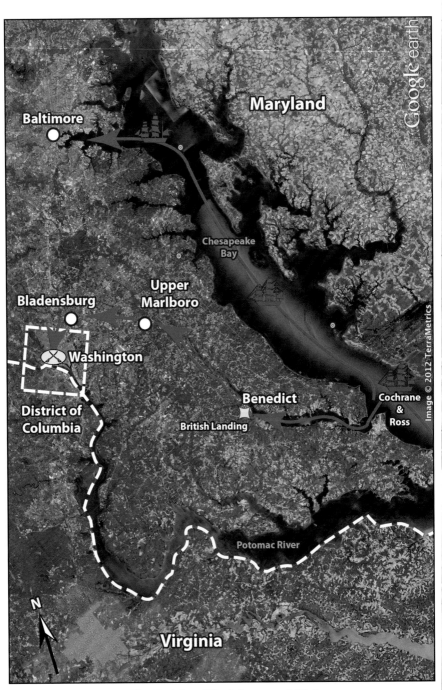

The Raid on Washington, 1814

The British Offensives, 1814

The defeat of Napoleon and his exile to Elba in the spring of 1814 allowed the British to turn their attention to North America. Large naval and land forces were sent west to bring an end to what Britain saw as American treachery. Four major operations were authorized: a punitive raid on Washington and Baltimore, the seizure of New Orleans, the occupation of northern Maine, and an advance into the Lake Champlain Valley. While troops sailed for Québec, Halifax, and Jamaica, the British cabinet instructed its negotiators, meeting with the American delegation in the Netherlands at Ghent, to demand a peace based on the conquests the British assumed would take place once their armies and fleets were assembled.

Vice Admiral Alexander Cochrane was placed in charge of operations in the Chesapeake Bay area. Determined to give the Americans "a complete drubbing before peace is made," he began the campaign with a proclamation encouraging African-American slaves, one-seventh of the American population, "to be received on board His Majesty's ships... or at military posts that may be established upon or near the coast of the United States when they will have the choice of entering with His Majesty's sea or land forces, or being sent as Free Settlers to the British possessions in North America or the West Indies..."

On 3 August 1814, Cochrane entered Chesapeake Bay, landing an army of some 4,000 men under Major-General Robert Ross, a veteran of Wellington's campaign in Spain. They quickly advanced on Washington. At Bladensburg the poorly organized American forces, largely recently enrolled militia,

A racist 1837 American political cartoon depicting British coercion of black and native populations in the War of 1812. The cartoon makes reference to the burning of Washington. [LAC C-040831]

History

abandoned a strong defensive position as soon as Congreve rockets were fired at them.

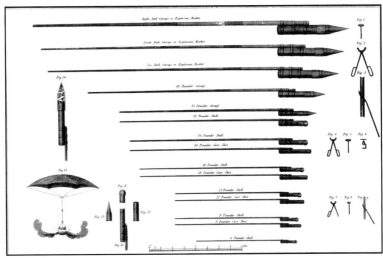

Congreve rockets, from a schematic by Sir William Congreve.

The advance on Washington resumed and Ross' battalions entered a town deserted by President Madison, his cabinet, and his army. The public buildings, including the White House, were set on fire. The British withdrew, rejoined Cochrane's ships, and prepared to threaten or, if circumstances were favourable, attack Baltimore – a much larger and better defended city.

The taking of the city of Washington in America. [LC USZ62-1939]

Ross was killed in the subsequent battle and, as Francis Scott Key's lyrics to the American national anthem correctly report, "the rockets red glare, the bombs bursting in air, gave proof through the night that our flag was still there…" The British commanders decided to call off what they insisted was a successful demonstration – not a failed attack – and sailed away to Jamaica.

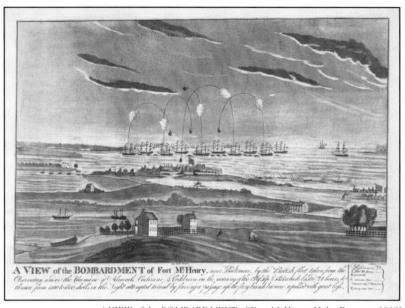

A VIEW of the BOMBARDMENT of Fort McHenry. [John Bower, c.1819]

British policy towards the American Northeast based on encouraging legitimate or illicit trade changed in 1814. Following the capture of Fort Sullivan and the village of Eastport without a shot fired in a joint operation led by Captain Sir Thomas Hardy, the late Lord Nelson's flag captain, and Lieutenant-Colonel Andrew Pilkington in July, Sir John Sherbrooke and Rear Admiral Edward Griffith landed an army of 2,000 regulars on the Maine coast at Castine on 1 September 1814. Their purpose was to gain control of the territory east of the Penobscot River, restoring eastern and northern Maine to British sovereignty and providing a more direct connection between the Maritimes and the Canadas. The garrison at the Fort on Castine Island fled after firing a single volley. The nearby village of Belfast showed no desire to resist the British and with the mouth of the river secured the troops, supported by elements of the fleet, moved along the river to seize the American frigate *Adams* which had sailed upstream to Hampden to avoid capture. The captain of the *Adams* had removed the ship's guns to help fortify the position but the local militia broke under rocket attack. The crew of the *Adams* burned the ship and withdrew to Bangor followed by Lieutenant-Colonel Henry John's infantry regiments. Bangor surrendered the next day.

The Assault at Castine, 1814

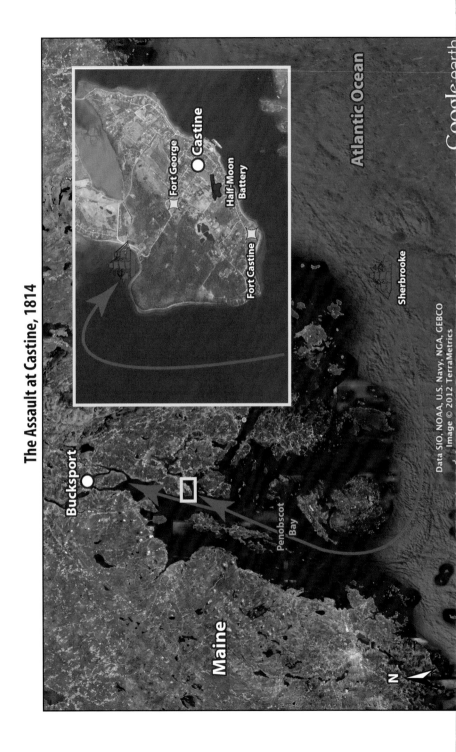

Data SIO, NOAA, U.S. Navy, NGA, GEBCO
Image © 2012 TerraMetrics

A second expeditionary force occupied Fort O'Brien and the village of Machias a week later, bringing the eastern Maine coast – one of the richest fishing and timber areas in North America – under British control. All males over 16 years living in the region were required to take an oath of allegiance to the King and most did so without objection. This part of the Commonwealth of Massachusetts (Maine became a state in 1820) had been heavily involved in trading with the British Empire throughout the war and few residents saw the British as foreign conquerors.

What remains of Fort O'Brien.

The third British operation of 1814 was organized in Lower Canada. Lord Bathurst, the Colonial Secretary, ordered Sir George Prévost to destroy the enemy's "naval establishments on Lake Erie and Lake Champlain" as well as Sackets Harbor. With the typical caution of a politician protecting himself from future criticism, Bathurst counselled Prévost to avoid any advance that might endanger "the safety of the force under your command."

A potential threat to Prévost's forces was the greatly strengthened American naval squadron on Lake Champlain. Captain Thomas Macdonough had selected the village of Vergennes, Vermont as a secure base where new ships and gunboats capable of regaining control of the Lake could be built. The *Saratoga*, 143 feet long with 26 heavy guns, was completed in just forty days. *Ticonderoga*, a civilian steamboat was converted into a 17-gun sloop. The 20-gun brig *Eagle*, the sloop *Preble*, and 12 gunboats achieved superiority over the British fleet, at least until *Confiance*, a new British frigate designed to carry 37 heavy guns, was launched at Île-aux-Noix.

Prévost's plans were constrained by enormous logistical problems. The arrival of 20,000 British troops, who had to be fed and quartered, strained the resources of the colony. The naval construction race on Lake Ontario presented another challenge. Building and equipping *HMS. St. Lawrence*, the 100-gun ship-of-the-line at Kingston, "absorbed the whole of the summer transport service from Montréal" leaving the quartermasters in Upper Canada short of provisions and ammunition for the army and its First Nations allies.

Logistics also determined that there would be no large scale transfer of newly arrived regiments to Kingston, never mind Niagara, and no major military operation in the area. The American fleet would abandon the lake once *St. Lawrence* was launched, but there were too few British troops at

History

The Naval Battle of Lake Champlain, 1814

Kingston to attack Sackets Harbor. The army in Lower Canada, as well as part of the civilian population, could be fed because droves of cattle as well as other supplies were pouring into the colony from Vermont and northern New York. Nothing could keep the farmers of the Champlain Valley from taking advantage of the high prices paid north of the border.

The British government had sent some of Wellington's best regiments and generals to Canada but Sir George Prévost, who had no significant operational experience, insisted on taking direct command of the large force set to invade the United States. Prévost's task was made much easier by the extraordinary decision to send a large part of the American army at Plattsburgh to Sackets Harbor. General Izard protested that "the enemy daily threatens an attack on my position at Champlain..." with a force "greatly superior to my own" but the Secretary of War, Armstrong, insisted, and Izard left Plattsburgh. His subordinate, Brigadier-General Alexander Macomb, was left to defend the town with less than 4,000 men.

Prévost began his campaign on 31 August; days after Izard's army had marched off to the west. Crossing the border with close to 10,000 men, Prévost issued a proclamation promising to protect "the peaceable and unoffending inhabitants...The enemy...was the government of the United States by whom this unjust and unprovoked war has been declared."

Prévost, without consulting the experienced brigadiers who would actually lead their men into battle, developed a plan which called for the fleet at Île-aux-Noix to play a major role in overcoming the Americans defending Plattsburgh. As commander-in-chief, Prévost could force the navy to cooperate and he ordered Captain George Downie, who had just arrived from Kingston to bring his ships south to support the attack. Downie

Macdonough's Victory on Lake Champlain, 11 September 1814. [LC DIG-pga-02823]

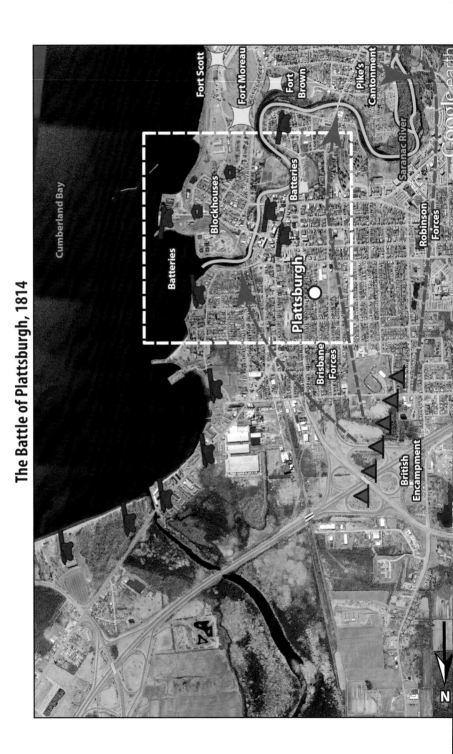

The Battle of Plattsburgh, 1814

protested that the recently built flagship *Confiance* was not ready to sail and its crew untrained but ultimately he followed orders.

The American defences were based on the Saranac River. Three earth-walled forts guarded the road (now Highway 9) that ran south along the lake and Macdonough's American naval squadron was anchored in Cumberland Bay protecting the right flank. This left the Americans vulnerable to an advance inland where their left flank could be turned by crossing the Saratoga River and rolling up the American positions from the rear. Recently mobilized militia from New York and Vermont were all that stood in the way.

Prévost's orders required Downie to attack the American fleet at the same time the army attacked on the morning of 11 September. Prévost believed that unless the American ships and gunboats were destroyed or scattered, their fire would prevent the army from taking the forts. This made little sense as the main effort across the Saranac was well inland and could not be affected by fire from gunboats in the bay. Downie compounded Prévost's misjudgements, discarding the advantage of a long-range action in which the heavier guns of *Confiance* would prevail and choosing instead to engage at close range. The result was an American victory. Downie was killed and *Confiance* struck its colours. Meanwhile, the leading elements of the Major-General Frederick Robinson's brigade had crossed the Saranac, scattering the militia. Robinson was bringing the rest of his men forward when an order to call off the attack arrived. Prévost decided that the naval defeat meant that "it was no longer prudent" to continue the action. The army was to return to Canada.

Robinson and his fellow officers were understandably outraged and their bitterness towards Prévost knew no bounds. During the withdrawal, morale and discipline suffered and more than 200 men deserted. News of the British defeat reached London at a time of growing difficulties with continental Allies meeting in Vienna and Prévost's actions helped persuade the British cabinet to end the war with America.

The Battle of Plattsburgh. [Lossing]

The Battle of New Orleans, 1814

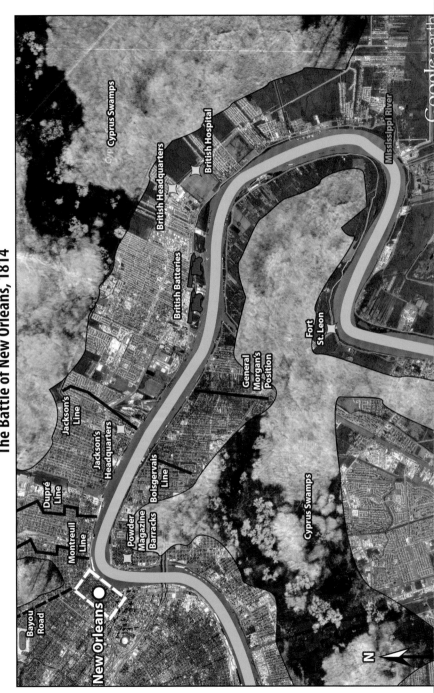

New Orleans

The plans to try and coerce the Americans into accepting British terms for ending the war by sending an expeditionary force to capture New Orleans were developed in August 1814. At that time, the British government appeared determined to force the Americans to accept recognition of a separate territory for the First Nations as well as a revision of the boundary between the United States and British North America. By 31 October, when Major-General Sir Edward Pakenham set sail for Jamaica, the British had abandoned plans to annex American territory and sacrificed the interests of a meaningless clause requiring respect for their First Nations allies, agreeing to settle for the restoration of their "rights, privileges, and possessions as they held them in 1811, before the commencement of the war." What then was the purpose of the attack on New Orleans? It seems likely that both the Prime Minister, Lord Liverpool, and the Duke of Wellington, Pakenham's brother-in-law, simply wished to avenge the failure at Plattsburgh and strike one last blow against the United States before ending the war.

Pakenham's army disembarked in Louisiana on 16 December 1814 and prepared to advance on New Orleans. They were at the end of a supply line that stretched back to Jamaica and ultimately England and were short of everything including proper clothes for the 1,100 black West Indian troops and cannon balls for the artillery. If a prompt attack had been possible, some success might have been achieved but two weeks passed before the army was ready to move and by then Major-General Andrew Jackson had organized a formidable mud-wall barrier with well-sited artillery.

The first British attack was called off when it became apparent that the mud-wall defensive works had survived a three-hour barrage. Four days later, faced with continuous rain, uncertain morale, and poor logistics, Pakenham was forced to fight or withdraw. He sent a large detachment across the Mississippi to capture the American guns dominating his left flank while West Indian

Andrew Jackson. [LC DIG-pga-00295]

troops tried to turn the other flank by working their way through a swamp. The infantry mounting the main frontal attack was to carry bundles of sugar cane to fill the ditch and ladders to scale the barrier wall. Everything that could go wrong did go wrong. The complex operation collapsed in confusion. Pakenham was killed and British losses – 251 killed, 1,259 wounded, and close to 500 taken prisoner – forced the British to retreat. Andrew Jackson wisely decided to declare victory and did not pursue the British who returned to their ships and sailed to Mobile Bay to reconsider their plans. After capturing a fort at the entrance to Mobile, an attack on the town and a further attempt on New Orleans was in preparation when on 12 February news of the war's end reached the British commander. The fleet and army returned to Jamaica.

Those who lost their lives at New Orleans were the victims of an ill-considered strategy as well as the slowness of communication. The British preferred to forget about the battle insisting it was meaningless because it occurred after the peace treaty was signed. The Americans took a very different view, constructing a memory of the war that linked the American victories at Plattsburgh and New Orleans with a peace treaty that restored the pre-war status quo. Andrew Jackson became a national hero and eventually President of the United States.

Battle of New Orleans and Death of Major-General Packenham, 8 January 1815. [William Edward West, 1816]

The Treaty of Ghent

Negotiations to bring an end to the war began in the town of Ghent, then part of the Netherlands, in the summer of 1814. The American delegation included Henry Clay, former Treasury Secretary Albert Gallatin, and John Quincy Adams; a future President. The British, pre-occupied with the complex task of laying the foundation for peace in Europe at the Congress of Vienna, sent an Undersecretary of State, Henry Goulburn, a retired admiral and legal specialist. Ghent was just two days travel from London and the British team maintained close contact with Prime Minister Lord Liverpool, the Secretary of State for War, the Earl of Bathurst, and the Foreign Secretary Lord Castlereagh.

The Americans had been instructed to secure an end to impressment, respect for neutral rights at sea, and to settle questions of damages and the exchange of prisoners of war. President Madison had added the suggestion that ceding all, or at least part, of Canada would be in Britain's best interest as a way of avoiding future conflict, but given the military situation, the American representatives decided not to mention this idea.

The British, confident that the naval and land forces being transferred to North America would change the balance of power, proposed far-reaching territorial changes including the establishment of a mutually guaranteed barrier state for the First Nations based on the Treaty of Greenville. The British also proposed a new boundary line giving parts of Maine and northern New York to Canada.

These proposals were immediately rejected by the American delegates who insisted that any buffer state or change in pre-war boundaries would violate American sovereignty. They claimed that the United States had never intended to conquer Canada and had always practiced the most humane and liberal policies towards the "indians" so there was no basis for British concern about the security of Canada or the future of American's First Nations. There was little point in further negotiation until the results of the British offensives were known. News of the burning of Washington was quickly followed by reports of the successful defence of Baltimore and the American victory on Lake Champlain. These events encouraged the Americans to argue for a peace agreement based on the pre-war status quo. They were willing to ignore the issue of impressment – the alleged cause of the war – since the defeat of Napoleon meant that the British Navy no longer needed every sailor they could find.

The British cabinet was less concerned with these American tactical victories, which they believed could be reversed in 1815, than with the situation in Europe. France was restive under the restored monarchy, and Russian determination to secure control of Poland had frustrated negotiations in Vienna. Liverpool asked Wellington to consider going to North America "with full powers to make peace or continue the war" but his government was really looking for a way out of the conflict. Wellington replied that if war broke out in Europe again, he would be needed there and that without naval superiority on the Lakes there was little that a North American army commander could do.

Wellington was right about the possibility of a new conflict in Europe but he knew little about the actual situation in Canada. The new British flagship on Lake Ontario, the *St. Lawrence*, guaranteed naval supremacy on Lake Ontario, threatening Sackets Harbor and much else. A more resolute commander in Lower Canada might easily win a second battle of Plattsburgh and with adequate time for logistical preparation, Amherstburg could be recovered in 1813. All of this and much else was possible because the American government was on the verge of financial collapse and the army suffering from shortages of supplies and manpower. Wellington knew even less about the far Northwest where Canadians and the First Nations of the Upper Mississippi had formed an effective alliance denying American access to the region between the river and Lake Michigan.

Lord Bathurst and others who favoured continuing the war were overruled when Castlereagh, increasingly troubled by reports of "the alarming situation in the interior of France" and the "unsatisfactory state of negotiations in Vienna" convinced the Prime Minister to end the war with America on almost any terms.

Neither Wellington nor Castlereagh had been party to any guarantees to the First Nations and were unwilling to press for any concession that might prolong the war. On Christmas Eve 1814, the Treaty of Ghent, restoring the status quo of 1812, was signed and sent to London and Washington for ratification.

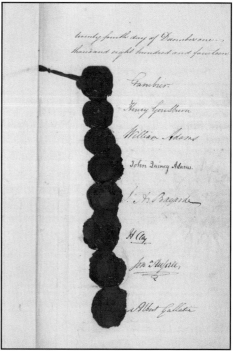

The Signatures on the Treaty of Ghent.
[William Edward West, 1816]

Peace

News of the peace agreement between Britain and the United States reached North America in February 1815. Professional officers of the British and American armies welcomed the news, paying courtesy visits to the encampments of men they had been planning to kill. Ordinary men and women, who lived in the borderlands where the war had devastated farms and villages breathed a sigh of relief and made plans to rebuild. The First Nations learned their fate the following month as the news reached the fur trade posts and forts in the upper Great Lakes and Mississippi Valley. At Prairie du Chien, Green Bay, Michlimackinac and other frontier communities, the warriors of the various Nations watched in dismay as the Canadian and British detachments withdrew. The promises of support for a protected First Nations territory had proved to be of little value.

Peace. [John Rubens Smith, LC-USZC4-3675]

The terms of the Treaty of Ghent called for the restoration of the 1783 border with a commission to arbitrate minor adjustments of the Maine-New Brunswick border. Initially the British negotiators at Ghent had argued that the American declaration of war in 1812 had abrogated the Treaty of Paris but they eventually accepted the American claim that the treaty signed in 1783 was "a permanent compact" establishing the American nation and "not liable, like ordinary treaties to be abrogated by a subsequent war between the parties." To be consistent, the Americans insisted that they had never planned to conquer and annex Canada, merely to force recognition of American rights at sea.

The British also conceded that American access to the fisheries in British waters was a permanent right recognized in 1783, not a concession made to establish good relations with the newly independent United States of America. It is evident that in 1814 as in 1783, the interests of the First Nations and the people of European descent living in British North America were sacrificed in the hope of establishing good relations between Britain and the United States.

This may well have been the best policy for the colonies that became the Dominion of Canada in 1867 as well as Britain. The original Thirteen Colonies that won their independence in 1783 were assuming control of most of the North American continent where vast tracks of arable land, a benign climate, and abundant resources offered endless development prospects. The population of the United States was growing at a phenomenal rate and its potential as a military power soon rivalled the major nations of Europe. Their imperialism was directed at First Nations, the Spanish in Florida, and ultimately Texas, the Southwest, California, and the Oregon country. It may reasonably be argued that if Canada was to emerge as a viable independent nation it had to avoid challenging America's "manifest destiny."

The fate of the First Nations living in territory claimed by the United States was to be even more desperate than their worst fears. The Second Treaty of Greenville imposed on the nations of the Ohio Valley in 1814 required acceptance of American sovereignty but avoided the issue of land transfers. Once the war ended a series of treaties obtained by threats, bribery, deception, and when required force, were signed allocating reserves in the least desirable areas to the various nations. During the 1830s the infamous removal acts forced the Cherokees, Creeks, and Chickshaws to move to Oklahoma. The forced "march" in 1838 known as the "Trail of Tears" was the most notorious of the removals but other First Nations suffered a similar situation. The First Nations north of the border were fewer in number but those who lived in the expanding area of settlement in Upper Canada were marginalized and confined to reserves. In the north and west, traditional patterns of First Nations life continued for another half-century.

The misery inflicted on the people of the Niagara region and other settlements in the Southwest contrasted sharply with the prosperity the war brought for others. Gerald Craig, author of *Upper Canada: The Formative Years*, notes that "large sums of (British) money had been spent to carry on the conflict… farmers had received high prices for their goods and merchants had flourished from the business of supplying the armed forces." With war's end, much of this activity ceased and a post-war recession began. Craig argues that the "political and psychological significance of the war proved to be far more significant than its physical effects." The political elite in Upper Canada, with the full support of successive British Governors, proposed laws limiting immigration from the United States relying on plans to divert British and especially Scottish immigrants to Canada. Military settlements of soldiers who had served in Canada were developed in the townships west of the Rideau River while independant British settlers occupied the more suitable townships further west.

Martello Tower in Saint John was not constructed until the aftermath of the War of 1812. [W. Hunt, LAC C-002981]

When the war ended, the British government was pre-occupied with its own problems including Napoleon's return and the Battle of Waterloo. After the defeat of Napoleon in 1815, fears that in a future war the Americans would seize control of the St. Lawrence River above Montréal led to the construction of the Rideau Canal linking Montréal with Kingston via the Ottawa River and the canal. The British taxpayer paid the full costs of this ambitious public works project as well as the new fortifications at Halifax, Saint John, Québec, Île-aux-Noix, Fort Wellington, Kingston, and elsewhere.

British garrisons were stationed throughout the colonies until 1863, providing economic stimulus as well as security.

The decision to negotiate an agreement to limit naval power on the Great Lakes, known as the Rush-Bagot Agreement of 1817, further enhanced the security of the Canadas and American pre-occupation with western expansion made a second invasion of Canada less and less likely. A few border skirmishes during the 1837-38 rebellions and the crisis atmosphere surrounding the dispute over the Oregon territory prompted further British investment in defensive works, transforming the rudimentary forts of 1812-14 into bastions of British power. Those who visit the ramparts at Québec, the defences of Halifax harbour, and the forts in Québec and Ontario are walking the sites of the 1812 war but exploring the military architecture of the mid 19th century – a physical legacy of the War of 1812.

The Anglo-American Convention of 1818 confirmed American access to the Newfoundland and Labrador coastal fisheries and fixed the boundary separating west of the Great Lakes at the 49th parallel, an enormous concession to the United States consistent with British policy in North America. The Convention also placed the Oregon territory under joint British and American rule until 1846. Demands for a border extending north to latitude 54 40 compelled British negotiators to accept a compromise based on extending the existing 49th parallel border except for Vancouver Island. Once again an agreement that met all reasonable American ambitions resolved a potentially dangerous conflict.

Survivors of the War of 1812. [LAC C-014466]

NEAR THIS SPOT
MAJOR GENERAL
SIR ISAAC BROCK K.C.B.
PROVISIONAL LIEUTENANT
GOVERNOR OF UPPER CANADA.
FELL ON 13TH OCTOBER 1812
WHILE ADVANCING TO REPEL
THE INVADING ENEMY.

Tour

The Legacy of 1812

This book was quite deliberately called *1812: A Guide to the War and its Legacy*. While the history section has provided readers with an understanding of the war, the tour section explores the legacy of 1812 – a memory that has been shaped and reshaped many times over the past 200 years. Many of the sites we send you to visit have been shaped time and again by the changing tides of memory.

War of 1812 Memorial in Toronto (1902). [City of Toronto Archives, f1257_s1057_it0188]

From the American perspective, the War of 1812 is merely one in a host of small scale wars in North America and the events of 1812-1815 are mostly forgotten in the collective memory of the United States. Other wars, which had clearer motivations or a more inspirational result, such as the Revolutionary War, the Civil War or the Second World War are all enshrined in the American historical narrative. Meanwhile, the War of 1812 with its complex politics of American aggression and unclear victories is easily pushed to the side. This was not always the case. It is clear that the Centennial celebrations in America took on more significance. In Sackets Harbor, then Assistant Secretary of the Navy, Franklin Delano Roosevelt, was on hand to unveil a monument in 1913. In Vergennes, Vermont where Macdonough built the American fleet that defeated the British on Lake Champlain, the 1914 celebrations drew large crowds. Perhaps more significant is that many of the defining symbols of American nationalism find their origin in the War of 1812. Samuel Wilson, a meat packing businessman from Troy, New

Tour

119

York supplied troop rations during the war and became the lasting personification of the government – today known as the ubiquitous Uncle Sam. The White House, which contrary to many myths was always white, faced its only attack by an invading army during the War of 1812. Finally, the lyrics of the "The Star Spangled Banner" were penned as 35-year-old Francis Scott Key watched the bombardment of Fort Henry aboard a neutral ship in the Chesapeake Bay. And yet, with the exception of Andrew Jackson's triumphant success at New Orleans, there are few battles or clear political consequences to the War of 1812 that remain entrenched in the American collective memory.

Uncle Sam, World War II. [LC-USZCA-599]

In Canada, the War of 1812 has taken on various meanings. In the immediate aftermath, the war became an inspiration to the citizens of Upper Canada who used the defence of the colony as an example of their loyalty and patriotism as British subjects. The losses and suffering of Upper Canadians connected the politics of the war to its personal and domestic consequences. For English Canadians, the War of 1812 reinforced their connection to the British Empire and became a foundational myth of Canada's national history until the 1960s. The story of the Canadian triumph over the invading Americans was personified by heroes of the war, like Sir Isaac Brock. Brock was revered as the epitome of self-sacrifice and virtuous service to the Empire and his heroic reputation would grow over the course of the 19th and 20th century. Alongside the "Loyalist" narrative of fleeing from the defeat of the British at the hands of American rebels, the War of 1812 provided a sort of redemption for those still loyal to British North America.

The hundredth anniversary celebrations again focused on these heroes of Upper (English) Canada and were mostly in Ontario for several important reasons. The descendants of the Upper Canadian Loyalists who had fled the United States and defended the colony in 1812 had also participated in the nation-building endeavour of Confederation, and their emerging sense of Canadian identity was incorporated with the narrative of the War of 1812. The role of the Canadian militia (though in reality limited during the conflict) was enshrined as evidence of the hardy nature of the Canadian character. The voluntary participation of Canadian soldiers in the Boer

Tour

War further cemented the concept of the country's militiamen as strong, noble and courageous. As well, unlike other Canadian provinces, Ontario could claim events, such as the Battle of Queenston Heights, Lundy's Lane, Crysler's Farm, and others, as sites of commemoration. It was on that 'sacred ground' where Upper Canadians had experienced the war's devastation but also where they had defended their nation. By the early 20th century, the sites were both traumatic and triumphant examples of Ontario's emergent Canadian nationalism and continued connection to the British Empire. At its hundredth anniversary, the War of 1812 stood as a testament to Ontario's narrative of Canadian history intertwined with its British Imperial past.

The 1914 designation of Fort Howe in Saint John, New Brunswick marked the beginning of an emerging system of heritage under the auspices of Parks Canada. In the wake of the First World War and the emergence of a new distinct Canadian identity, the Historic Sites and Monuments Board of Canada was officially established in 1919. The board existed to recognize and designate sites of national historical significance. Its first chairman was Brigadier General E.A. Cruikshank, a noted authority on the War of 1812. He and the majority of his colleagues were heavily influenced by the Loyalist history and as a result the board's agenda largely focused on the commemoration of the great men and battles credited with establishing the nation. A lack of resources limited the board's activities to simply designating sites, leaving the focus on commemoration rather than preservation. Sites received a maroon and bronze plaque or stone cairn, though at times the board supported community-led movements to commission substantial monuments at the most symbolic battle grounds. At its 1920 annual meeting, the Board approved 25 sites for commemoration, 14 of which were located in Ontario and nine that were related to the War of 1812. By 1930, the number

Notice the maroon and gold Historic Sites and Monuments Board plaque at the Drummond Hill Cemetery. [Caitlin McWilliams]

of sites commemorating the War of 1812 had grown to 38. Today, the Historic Sites and Monuments Board has designated over 70 historic sites related to the War of 1812. Of these, 81% were approved by the Board during Cruikshank's tenure as chairman. For this reason, the War of 1812 stands as the most commemorated event by the Historic Sites and Monuments Board in Canadian history.

As you tour the sites and read the plaques dedicated to the War of 1812, be sure to note when it was dedicated and by whom. Following the Great Depression, the Historic Sites and Monuments Board emphasized commemoration over preservation. This change was most visible in Ontario where fortifications and historic houses were fully restored so that they could be opened to the public. In Ontario, you will also come across plaques and markers posted by the Ontario Heritage Foundation. The foundation was originally known as the Archaeological and Historic Sites Board until 1968 when it became an agency of the Ontario Ministry of Tourism and Culture. It is responsible for protecting, preserving, and promoting the built, natural and cultural heritage of Ontario. Its most recognizable work is the Provincial Plaque Program which has placed over 1,200 blue and gold plaques throughout Ontario.

The bicentennial celebrations have sought to create a new, and equally simplistic, version of events between 1812 and 1815. The story in 2012 seeks to unite the entire country of Canada in a celebration of a nation-building experience. It places the experience of French *Canadians*, British Redcoats, the Canadian militia and Aboriginals side by side, all acting together to repel invading American forces. Much like Ontario's focus on its own war narrative in 1912, the War of 1812 in 2012 has concentrated on specific events and parts of the war to communicate a clear, unambiguous narrative. In reality, the cooperation of those groups relied on a complex mix of promises, motivations, and politics between all of the interested parties fighting against northern American expansion. Their incomplete victory in 1815 won Canada the right not to be American, but little else. The 2012 official Canadian government version of events also promotes the idea of a war that spawned 200 years of peace between the two countries. Yet, many of the fortifications that

Tecumseh 25 cent piece. [mint.ca]

stand today were strengthened, expanded, or even built entirely in the years following the Treaty of Ghent in 1815. Most of the sites you will visit on this tour reflect the physical legacy of the War of 1812 through Britain's attempts to fortify the border against future American invasions.

Battlefield touring is always, to a large degree, driven by what you can see and visit. The emergence of Toronto from the waterfront village of York to the economic hub of Canada has completely changed the physical and figurative landscape, and with it our ability to fully understand the burning of the city in 1813. Toronto is an extreme example where at least Fort York remains. Other places like Crysler's Farm, which now sits under the waters of the St. Lawrence after the seaway expansion, are of use only to witness the construction of memory rather than understanding the landscape of battle. Visiting the sites of 1812 with this guide will give you some sense of the mixture of historical interpretation and imperfect memory that remains today. This, of course, is not terribly different than touring the Canadian battlefields of Europe. But following in the footsteps of soldiers who fought in skirmishes and pitched battles 200 years ago over vastly different landscapes has an added measure of difficulty. Quite aside from the landscape, it is difficult to grasp pre-industrialized warfare in the age of sail, horses, muskets and cannons. The history section has highlighted the realities of war in 1812 and sought highlight life and conflict in the early 19th century. It will be your task to get past the images and historical legacy of warfare in the 20th century so that those who fought in the War of 1812 are understood on their terms.

On a practical note, following the footsteps of those who fought more than 200 years ago will take you to places you likely would never have visited. These sites are normally located around cities far more important in the 19th century than they are today. Unlike the European battlefields, modern amenities are never far from these sites. We have tried to make reference to other potential stops where possible but we strongly suggest you research the areas you choose to stay. Many times, the monuments or museums will not fill your days and there is plenty to visit in every town and city we take you. A final note on the maps – we have laid out a Google map for you to follow but we have also added GPS coordinates and highly suggest you follow a GPS unit or familiarize yourself with a good set of maps. There is simply no way, in a guide like this, to provide comprehensive maps.

The content of the tour section has been influenced by the quality of the information available on the internet. All of the better known historical sites have a well-developed web presence which can be easily accessed through a quick search. We have, therefore, devoted more space to lesser known and isolated places of interest. Visit the main Parks Canada website at pc.gc.ca for more information. For sites in the United States visit nps.gov.

Touring Southwestern Ontario and the Northern United States

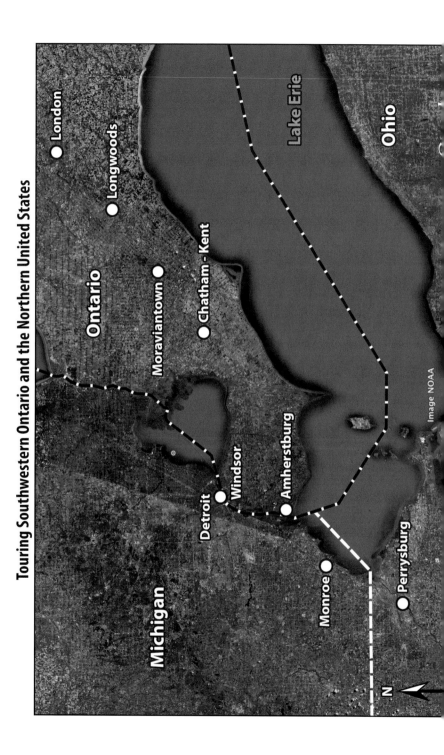

Touring Southwestern Ontario & the Northern United States

Your tour of Southwestern Ontario will take you through the London and Chatham areas, but the majority of the sites are located in the Essex County region. The area is the oldest continually inhabited European settlement in Canada west of Montréal. Though strained throughout the War of 1812, the relationship between the two border cities of Windsor and Detroit, Michigan has become the foundation of the city's well-established tourism industry and economy. The Ambassador Bridge opened in 1929 and is the busiest international border crossing in North America. The Windsor-Detroit Tunnel, opened one year later, is the second, and together the two connections allow about 300,000 people to cross between the countries every day. This bilateral relationship helps support Windsor and Detroit's lively downtown cores and provides easy access to cross-border shopping, travel, and entertainment. Views of the Windsor-Detroit skyline can be enjoyed on a walk or bike along the Riverwalk Trail, a 10km park stretching along the riverfront from the foot of the Ambassador Bridge to Hiram Walker's Canadian Club distillery. Other downtown attractions include Caesar's Windsor Hotel and Casino, Hiram Walker's distillery, and the Art Gallery of Windsor. If possible, visit Windsor during the annual two-week Summerfest during which one of the world's largest firework displays is launched over the Detroit River.

The Ambassador Bridge connecting Windsor and Detroit. [Caitlin McWilliams]

London & Chatham-Kent

Longwoods & Chatham-Kent

(A) The first stop on the London to Chatham tour takes you to the cairn that commemorates the Battle of Longwoods, 4 March 1814. (*GPS – Battle Hill National Historic Site, 2945 Longwoods Rd. Southwest Middlesex, Ontario*) From Toronto drive west on Highway 401 past London and take the 402 west toward Sarnia for 17km. Take Exit 86 to Longwoods Rd. The memorial is on your left. The 1814 skirmish between elements of the 24th and 28th U.S. Regiments and a detachment of British troops (Royal Scots, 89th Foot, McGregor's Kent Volunteers and Caldwells Rangers) was one of several encounter battles fought in the area after the American victory at the Battle of the Thames in October 1813. All of Southwestern Ontario from Amherstburg east to the Grand River Valley was a kind of "no man's land" in 1814 as neither side maintained permanent garrisons between Burlington Heights and Fort Malden.

At Longwoods the American commander Captain A.H. Holmes established log breastworks on the west side of 20 mile ravine. Apparently the senior British officer, Captain James Badsen, underestimated the strength of the American position and decided to attack before night fell. Moving down the eastern slope of the ravine the British were subjected to withering fire and tried to move north to outflank the enemy. Darkness saved them from a truly desperate situation. The American losses were seven men wounded while the British reported fourteen killed and 31 wounded.

Battle Hill Memorial at Longwoods. [Caitlin McWilliams]

Tour

It is possible to walk the ground over which the battle was fought and if you do you will no doubt wonder how Captain Badsen could possibly have blundered so badly. The Historic Sites and Monument Board of Canada designated the Battle of Longwoods as a National Historic Site in 1924. The memorial plaque was added in 1929 and the site sits on high ground just east of what is now called "Battlefield Creek." Historically, the Upper Thames Military Re-enactment Society recreates the battle on the first weekend of May at the Longwoods Conservation Area. (*GPS – 8348 Longwoods Rd. Thamesville, ON*) For more information see royal-scots.com.

The Upper Thames Military Re-enactment Society in action, May 2012. [Nick Lachance]

(B) From the Battle of Longwoods monument continue west on Longwoods Rd. to the Fairfield on the Thames National Historic Site of Canada and the Fairfield Museum. (*GPS – 14878 Longwoods Rd. Thamesville, ON*) In Fairfield, Moravian missionaries established a settlement for Christianized natives chiefly from the Delaware First Nations. The Moravians, a German-speaking pacifist sect, left the United States after the Revolutionary War to create a new mission town in Upper Canada, which by 1813 included fifty homes, a two-story church and two schools. It was the largest and most productive settlement in the Thames valley. After the American victory at the Battle of the Thames in 1813, Fairfield was looted and burned to the ground by William Harrison's American militia who claimed that some of the residents had fought alongside Tecumseh and others had hidden British soldiers. After the war New Fairfield, later named Moraviantown, was rebuilt on the south bank of the river.

Today the Fairfield on the Thames National Historic Site preserves the outline of the original village in the fields beside the museum and monument. The museum is seasonally open May through October, Tuesday to Saturday from 10:00 to 17:00 and Sunday 01:00 to 17:00. The museum displays artefacts dug up from the site of the village, details the history of Aboriginal cultures and houses an array of objects from the War of 1812. Be sure to sign the guestbook, which dates back to 1960, and browse the small one-room exhibit. Though there are no panels explaining what you are

The Fairfield Museum is a quaint museum with a number of unique artefacts, including these arrowheads dating back to the battle and the aboriginal settlement that was burned by the Americans in 1814. [Nick Lachance]

Tour

seeing, the museum still offers a fascinating glimpse into the preservation of local history. Its commemoration of the destruction of Fairfield reveals a local legacy of the war that might be easy to overlook. It offers one answer to the question of how small southern Ontario communities recovered from the devastating effects of the War of 1812. Some rebuilt, others moved, and many memorialized their experience in different forms.

(C) Leave Fairfield and continue southwest 2.5km along Longwoods Rd. to the well-kept National Historic Persons Site with a magnificent monument honouring Tecumseh. (*GPS – Longwoods Rd. Thamesville, ON*) Under a program called the Persons of National Historic Significance, individuals can be nominated 25 years after their death. Parks Canada administers the program and maintains the monuments and plaques that are located in areas significant to the person. The monument honouring Tecumseh was erected in 1931 with a brief description of his life and a likeness in a stone etching. The memorial is close to the actual battlefield but the changed landscape makes it virtually impossible to pinpoint the exact location of the Battle of Moraviantown. Forests and marshes have been replaced with highways and farmer's fields. The battle took place as the British army retreated along what is now Longwoods Road, with the river on one side, and their First Nations allies in the trees and marshes on the other. What you can clearly see today is that when they did face their American pursuers, there was little room to manoeuvre.

Tecumseh was made a Person of National Significance by the Historic Sites and Monuments Board of Canada in 1931. The original monument [right] is weather worn and completely unreadable. The 1931 monument gives a brief bio of the life and times of Tecumseh. [Nick Lachance]

Chatham-Kent

D On a nice day, lunch in Chatham's Tecumseh Park Armory is a lovely mid-day stop. (*GPS – Tecumseh Park Armory, Stanley St. Chatham, ON*) From Longwoods Rd. turn right on Thames St. and then left on King St. West. For those interested in the memorials of the First and Second World Wars, the Chatham-Kent Memorial is on your right just short of the mall. King St. West is has abundant parking and is only a short distance from the main 1812 sites.

Cross the Thames River and take a stroll through Tecumseh Park Armory. The park was the location of a small skirmish between Aboriginal forces led by Tecumseh and American forces as they retreated from southern Ontario in 1813. It has a small plaque to Tecumseh and a canon from the era at the western most tip of the park. On your way you will pass a monument honouring 200 years of the Essex Regiment 1792-1992.

E The local museum in Chatham has several displays devoted to the War of 1812 and includes many useful local maps and interesting paintings of the period. (*GPS – 75 Williams St. North. Chatham, ON*) Their exhibit for the War of 1812, "Our Winnerless Victory," serves as another reminder of the terrible cost of the war for southern Ontario's small communities. Chatham is devoted to their local hero from the war, John McGregor. A politician and businessman, McGregor joined the militia as a Lieutenant in 1812 despite being 61 years of age. At nearby Longwoods, he lost his arm fighting the Americans and was promoted to Captain a few months later. The Chatham museum highlights the location of his mill, which was once the backbone of the local economy, and his service in defence of Southern Ontario.

Tour

Tour

Amherstburg & Fort Malden

Windsor

20

Fort Malden
National Historic
Site

(A)

Laird Avenue South

Dalhousie Street

Sandwich Street North

Amherstburg

Amherstburg
Soldier's
Monument

Gore Street

(C)

King's Navy Yard
Park

(B)

Lake Erie

N

Amherstburg & Fort Malden

(A) The drive to Fort Malden in Amherstburg is all about the last 30 minutes. (*GPS – 100 Laird Ave. South. Amherstburg, ON*) From Chatham make your way back to the 401 West and continue through the nondescript, flat Ontario landscape to Windsor. Continue onto Talbot Rd. and then immediately turn left onto Howard Ave. From Howard, turn right onto North Townline

Rd. and continue onto Malden Rd. until you reach Front Rd. North and turn left onto the scenic route along the Detroit River. The half hour drive of 10km along the river is a relaxing way to approach historic Fort Malden. Take a right on Maple Ave. and you will reach your destination.

The modern river has bridges spanning it, but in 1812 it remained an imposing obstacle for British and American armies. Upon reaching downtown Amherstburg where Fort Malden is located, it quickly becomes clear that the town is geared towards tourists. If you have the time, stop at one of the many restaurants for lunch or an ice cream. Hopefully the sun is shining and you can enjoy walking through the town's beautiful parks and gardens.

It was at Fort Malden where the British armies defending Southwestern Ontario were stationed. Today, only the outline of the structure remains, as it was burned by American soldiers in 1813 as they advanced into Ontario.

The grounds at Fort Malden. [Nick Lachance]

The modern fort that stands before you is more reminiscent of the rebuilt fortification after the war and throughout the rest of the 19th century. You can learn about the Fort's history at the Visitor's Centre or by taking a tour hosted by the enthusiastic staff.

Standing within the walls of the fort, it is easy to understand its purpose. The commanding view of the Detroit River revealed any ship movement and the cannons ensured control of the waterway. Deep gullies reveal the old walls of the Fort and suggest the defensive nature of the structure. Heavy wooden palisades crested the top of these manmade slopes. Although the War of 1812 forts did not approach the complexity or security of the stone fortresses of Europe, they were still an imposing obstacle for the common foot soldier.

(B) A short distance from Fort Malden sits the Amherstburg Navy Yard National Historic Site. (*GPS – 214 Dalhousie St. Amherstburg, ON*) Continue south on Laird Ave. then take a right on Fort Malden Dr. and a left on Dalhousie St. Prior to the War of 1812, the naval yard served as the shipbuilding facility for the Provincial Marine, allowing for the transportation of the British army around the colony. During the war, the navy yard became the base of operations on Lake Erie. Following Oliver Perry's victory on Lake Erie September 1813, Amherstburg was abandoned. It was designated a site of national significance in 1928.

Adjacent to the Park House Museum at the north end of the park are two monuments that honour those who fought during the Battle of Lake Erie. The first is a four-sided pillar that displays four Historic Sites and Monuments Board plaques. The plaques commemorate those killed in action and offer

The monument at the Navy Yard. [Caitlin McWilliams]

The blue roof guides the way to the Bois Blanc Blockhouse. [Caitlin McWilliams]

Walk through the marina until you reach the 375-foot tall Sky Tower. From this point there are three trails that run south and meet at the blockhouse, so take your time walking and enjoy the island. The middle trail is the one which runs through the majority of the abandoned amusement park structures. The blockhouse is near the far tip of the island but is easy to spot because of its blue roof. The white lighthouse is not far behind. Note that its lamp was destroyed in 1954 when vandals started a fire.

Boblo Island retains an aura of mystery and intrigue because of its use as an amusement park from 1898 to 1933. Midst overgrown grass and creeping vines are a number of structures left from the era, including the large Dance Pavillion, Carousel Building, Powerhouse, and a mini putt course. "Private property. No trespassing" signs forbid entry into the dilapidated buildings, but visitors will enjoy exploring the colorful grounds nonetheless. While walking you may also want to visit the Sailor's Monument on the eastern shore of the island.

Tour

137

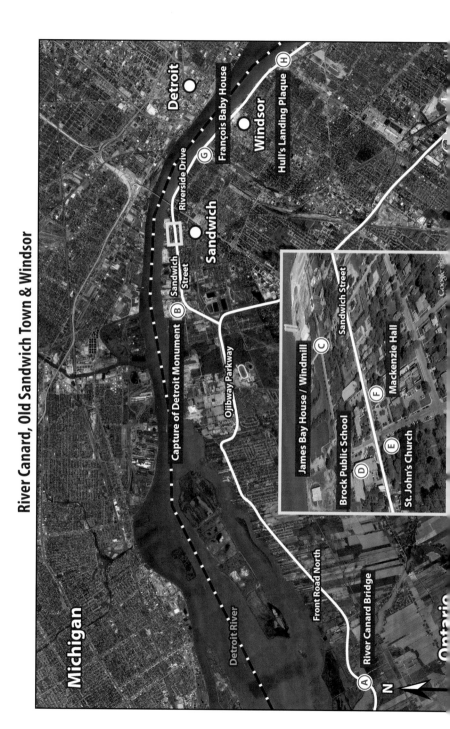

Tour

River Canard, Old Sandwich Town & Windsor

Michigan

Detroit River

Front Road North

A River Canard Bridge

N

Ontario

Ojibway Parkway

Capture of Detroit Monument

B

Sandwich Street

Sandwich

Riverside Drive

G

François Baby House

Windsor

H

Hull's Landing Plaque

Detroit

James Bay House / Windmill

C

Sandwich Street

Brock Public School

D

E St. John's Church

F Mackenzie Hall

Touring River Canard, Old Sandwich Town & Windsor

The Windsor-Essex County region is steeped in the history of the War of 1812. Fort Malden is arguably the most popular site in the area, however it worthwhile to spend a day exploring some of the lesser known sites in the Windsor area. The route, from Fort Malden to Windsor with stops in River Canard (Amherstburg / La Salle) and Sandwich, is an easy and scenic drive along the waterfront. Most of the tour stops are only a short distance from the main road.

On 12 July 1812, Hull and his army invaded Canada at Sandwich and headed south along the Detroit River towards Fort Malden. The skirmishes at River Canard were one of the first acts of resistance to American invasion and culminated on 16 July at the bridge over River Canard, halfway between Sandwich (14km) and Amherstburg (10km). A force of 280 American troops outnumbered roughly 60 British regulars, Native allies, and Essex Militia, who fell back towards the fort. After ten days of intermittent fighting, Hull retreated to Detroit and the British reoccupied the post.

(A) Your first stop is the provincial plaque marking the location of the old wooden bridge that today stands beside a concrete bridge marking the skirmishes at the Canard River. (*GPS – 1498 County Rd. 20. Amherstburg, ON*) The plaque is not visible from the road and if you are not careful you might miss this quick stop. From Amherstburg head north on Sandwich St. S / County Rd. 20 which turns into Front Rd. Drive about 10km and pass over the Canard River. Be on the lookout for the blue signs for "Hancock & Dean Bridge to Nationhood." The bridge was recently renamed

The Government of Ontario plaque by the Canard River. [Caitlin McWilliams]

Tour

to commemorate two British soldiers: James Hancock, who was the first British soldier to die during the War of 1812, and John Dean, who was wounded and taken prisoner. Cross the bridge and immediately turn left on the dirt road along the riverbank to where the plaque stands.

The Canard Valley is a mix of unspoiled countryside and marshland and there are various spots along the river for relaxing, portaging, camping, or just to stop for a picnic. The river is also great spot for fishing and is famous locally for its thriving catfish population. Adventurous or outdoorsy types may choose to tour the site by water, and between April and November, canoes and kayaks are available to rent from the River Canard Canoeing Company. The rental company operates out of a farm which also features ice cream shop, store, and petting zoo. In the winter months you can traverse the area on foot by indulging in the Canadian tradition of snowshoeing. See windsoressex.com for more information.

B From River Canard move along to Sandwich, a historic township in Windsor where Hull invaded Upper Canada and a number of famous British generals took up headquarters. Sandwich is one of the oldest settlements in Ontario and has done much to retain its connection to the War of 1812. From River Canard, continue on Front Rd., passing through Lasalle and enter Windsor. Here the road turns into Ojibway Pwky. Note that you must follow the sign which tells you to turn left or you will end up on the expressway. At the intersection of Sandwich St. and Ojibway Pwky. you might choose to stop briefly and read the plaque describing the capture of Detroit. (*GPS – 4110 Sandwich St. Windsor, ON*) The pyramid-shaped marker is on the left side of the intersection on a slight bend just past the

The Government of Canada Monument describing the capture of Detroit. [Caitlin McWilliams]

Tour

water reclamation plant, and you can park on the dirt road behind the marker.

From painting murals on the sides of buildings to restored period houses and the streets named after wartime generals, the tour of downtown Sandwich sets up nicely for a leisurely walk in a quaint historic neighbourhood. Allow yourself an hour or so to take in the historic sites.

(C) In Sandwich, stop first at the James Duff-Baby House and interpretation centre (*GPS – 221 Mill St. Windsor, ON*), run in partnership with the François Baby House in Windsor. Built in 1798, the house is considered the oldest building in Windsor and retains its original orientation to the Detroit River. Before the skirmishes at River Canard, General Hull invaded Sandwich and commandeered the house of local militia man James Duff-Baby as his headquarters. When he retreated, General Brock, Colonel Proctor, and General Harrison subsequently occupied it. One of the great stories to come out of the war is that Duff-Baby is reputed to have hosted a dinner in the house attended by the Shawnee Chief Tecumseh and Proctor. Though damaged, the house survived the attack, occupation, and looting by American troops and has been restored to reflect how it looked during the early 19th century. The house is now owned by the Ministries of Culture and Citizenship and is only open to the public for special events. The interpretation centre, located behind the house, is open on a more frequent, if sporadic, basis and displays artefacts found on archeological digs of the site. Across the street in Mill Park is a replica of a windmill used by James Duff-Baby's, and whose flour was commandeered by Hull for his soldiers.

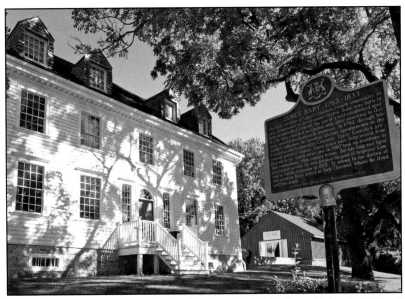

The front facade of the James Duff-Baby House. [Caitlin McWilliams]

(D) Walk down Russell St. past Brock Park, and up Brock St. At the intersection of Brock St. and Sandwich St. there are a few historic buildings with ties to the War of 1812 each with plaques describing their significance. On the west corner is the former Stone College School founded in 1797. The school served as reserve barracks during the war. It is now General Brock Public School and the Windsor Public Library. (*GPS – 221 Brock St. Windsor, ON*)

(E) On the south corner is St. John's Anglican Church and churchyard, a Gothic-style church rebuilt in 1819 to replace the building burned by invading Americans during the war. (*GPS – 3314 Sandwich St. Windsor, ON*) The graveyard contains gravestones dating from the 18th century.

(F) Slightly further north is the Windsor jail and Mackenzie Hall, the former Essex County Courthouse. (*GPS – 3261 Sandwich St. Windsor, ON*) The structure was the fourth courthouse built on the site, one of which was also burned down during the American invasion. It now functions as a cultural centre.

Sandwich has a few great places to stop for lunch. The Dominion House (*GPS – 3140 Sandwich St. Windsor, ON*) is a local favourite where you can enjoy classic pub fare in the oldest tavern in the Border Region. Rock Bottom Bar & Grill (*GPS – 3236 Sandwich St. Windsor, ON*) is a reliable "go to" establishment, mainly because of their casual atmosphere, tasty food, and 30 kinds of beer. For a delicious selection of baked goods, do not miss the McGregor-Cowan House (*GPS – 3118 Sandwich St. Windsor, ON*), the second oldest building in Windsor and indulge in homemade pies, sweets, and more.

(G) From Sandwich, take Riverside Dr. West towards the François Baby House, a two-storey brick building located in downtown Windsor. (*GPS – 272 Pitt St. Windsor, ON*) The site was a key stepping off point for both the American invasion of Upper Canada and the subsequent British capture of Detroit. During the war, the property was occupied by the armies of General Hull and General Brock, and the house has survived as a national heritage site owned by the City of Windsor. It is the current home of Windsor's Community Museum which is commemorating the bicentennial through exhibits, open houses, and a garden dedication.

In the spring of 1812, François Baby, a prominent local citizen, began building a house near the shore of the Detroit River. On 12 July, the American army invaded Canada at Sandwich and General William Hull and his soldiers occupied the Baby property, converting his 8km ribbon farm into a fortified defence. The position of the house was crucial. It was an ideal location to plan an invasion of Fort Malden and strategically, the house sat directly opposite to Fort Lernoult in Detroit. Soldiers pitched their tents in Baby's orchards while senior officers occupied and pillaged the partially constructed home. After a number of indecisive skirmishes with British outposts along the Canard River, Hull retreated. The house was taken over by Major General Isaac Brock, and it was from this location that he began the artillery bombardment that ultimately led to the surrender of Detroit.

Over the last two hundred years, the François Baby House has undergone numerous modifications and repairs. As a result, much of the original 1812 structure has been lost or compromised. Restoration of the house began in 1948 and the exterior has since been restored to look like it did in 1812 with one exception – the front facade originally faced north toward the river. What remains of the original framework is its rubble foundation, the back of the fireplace in the basement, two end walls, a majority of the north wall, and the supporting wooden timber under the north entrance – all of which are visible today. Unlike the exterior of the home, the interior does not resemble a 17th century dwelling. Instead, the space has been modernized to accommodate offices and exhibits with the original structural elements incorporated into the design.

A photograph of the François Baby House from the air shows how time and modernization has dwarfed the 1812 settlement. [Caitlin McWilliams]

Encroaching urban development has all but erased the small house which, over time, has become dwarfed by large modern buildings on all sides. The museum sees thousands of visitors annually and is supported by a thriving volunteer group, *Les amis Duff-Bâby*. Still, this historical gem is tucked humbly into the city's downtown landscape and is often missed by tourists or goes unnoticed by locals. Discussions have proposed moving the house to a more prominent location, but the historical value of the location and its ties to the opening of the War of 1812 has kept it on its original plot.

Visitors to the site will notice the familiar Ontario plaque near the front right of the house. Behind the house is the well-manicured François Baby Peace Garden. The garden is part of a network of twenty-three across the southern Great Lakes region. The new crossborder Peace Garden Trail was launched in honour of the Bicentennial of the War of 1812.

The museum houses over 10,000 artefacts plus extensive holdings of maps, photographs, and documents which focus on the history of French, British, Aboriginals, African-American and other cultural groups from Windsor-Essex County, from 1701 to the present. Each year, the museum mounts approximately four rotating exhibits and is currently highlighting "Living in 1812: Life on the Sandwich Frontier" until the Fall of 2013. Through panels and artefacts, the former offers a critical analysis into the opening of the War of 1812 and details the property's role at the forefront of the conflict. Highlights include cannonballs found on the site that support the house's role in the capture of Detroit, and a flag of the 1812 period that was acquired with the story that it covered Tecumseh's body after he died. The museum is self-directed but there is always staff on hand to answer any questions. Bilingual guides are available. The site is wheelchair accessible and there is a stairlift to the upper floor. School group tours are offered and should be booked ahead by calling (519)-253-1812. General admission is free, though a donation is much appreciated. Parking is located on the road in front of the museum.

Cannonballs from the War of 1812 at the François Baby House. [Caitlin McWilliams]

An aerial view of the Detroit River from the Canadian side. [Caitlin McWilliams]

Visitors researching the War of 1812 will find their extensive collection of militia-based microfilm of interest, as well as a wealth of secondary sources. Researchers are advised to make an appointment before visiting. For more information on the François Baby House or Windsor's role during the War of 1812, see *Mansion to Museum: The François Baby House and Its Times* by R. Alan Douglas.

After the tour, you are encouraged to explore Windsor's lively downtown core. Enjoy a walk or bike ride along the Riverwalk Trail, a 10km park stretching along the riverfront from the foot of the Ambassador Bridge to Hiram Walker's Canadian Club distillery. Highlights of the trail, in addition to a spectacular view of the Windsor-Detroit border, include the Windsor Sculpture Park, Dieppe Gardens, various war memorials, and The Spirit of Windsor, an old CN steam engine. There are intermittent parking lots along the way, coin-operated viewfinders for peering at passing freighters or across to Detroit, and The Bistro restaurant at Ouellette Ave.

(H) If you choose to walk east along the Riverfront Trail, note that there is an Ontario Archaeological and Historic Sites Board plaque commemorating Hull's landing of 12 July 1812, located on the north side of Riverside Dr. East at the traffic light west of Walker Rd. (*GPS – 1950 Riverside Dr. East. Windsor, ON*)

If possible, visit Windsor during the annual two-week Summerfest during where one of the world's largest firework displays is launched over the Detroit River. Regardless of when you visit, we recommend you stay at the Windsor Riverside Inn (*GPS – 333 Riverside Dr. West. Windsor, ON*) located adjacent to the François Baby House and a three minute walk from the main downtown road. Be sure to ask for a room facing the water!

Tour

Monroe, Michigan & the River Raisin Massacre

Crossing the Border: Michigan & Ohio

(A) Begin your trip to the battlefields of northern Ohio and Michigan at the River Raisin National Battlefield Park in Monroe. (*GPS – 1403 East Elm Ave. Monroe, MI*) To get to Monroe (formerly Frenchtown after its original French settlers) take exit 13 off the I-75 and you will arrive on East Elm Ave., 500 metres from the park. The battle of River Raisin in January 1813 is far better known among Americans than Canadians. The cry "Remember the Raisin" was heard throughout the rest of the war. British General George Prévost withdrew after defeating the Americans there, and left their wounded to his First Nations allies, who believed that wounded soldiers deserved death. The unnecessary killing of the wounded soldiers inspired the American battle cry, which was used at the battle of Moraviantown where the Americans avenged the wounded soldiers killed here. It also transformed the memory of the war in the United States from an offensive attack against Canada to a defensive one. "Remember the Raisin" was equally about remembering the attack on American soil and the frontier settlements of Michigan and Ohio.

You will notice quickly that the town of Monroe has many signs noting historic events, though not all from the War of 1812. Still small to this day, you can still walk the streets that formed the border of Frenchtown in the centre of town on the north side of the river.

The River Raisin Battlefield Park Information Center. [Nick Lachance]

The River Raisin Battlefield National Park sits next to the river and looking from the parking lot across the water, you can see the spot where the Americans retreated from advancing British forces. All of this is also adroitly presented on plaques in front of the building. This newly created national park looks small, but offers excellent information on the timeline and events of the River Raisin battle. The staff is friendly, helpful and worth talking to when you are browsing their exhibits. Be certain to sit down for the "light show" that illustrates British and American troop movements across the River Raisin landscape and their battles. The Visitor Centre also holds a painting by Tim Kurtz of Frenchtown as it was when the battle over the River Raisin was fought. In addition to the National Park, you may also wish to visit Monroe's local museum which has information about the town's history before and after the War of 1812. (*GPS – 126 South Monroe St. Monroe, MI*)

B Continuing north on East Elm Ave. will take you by more of the original River Raisin battlefield. (*GPS – 1323 East Elm Ave. Monroe, MI*) Less than a minute's drive from the National Park, the land is currently in an undeveloped state but there are future plans to expand the existing battlefield park and revitalize the original site of Frenchtown. On your right there will be a place to pull over safely where you can find a sign commemorating the River Raisin battle, but little else marks the site. However looking to the grove of trees in the distance you can easily imagine how helpless the inhabitants of Frenchtown must have felt, watching British Red Coats and Native warriors advance across the frozen open ground towards their little village.

The River Raisin Battlefield sites, one of the few remaining unaltered 1812 battlefield sites you can visit. [Nick Lachance]

C Directly adjacent to the undeveloped battlefield is the River Raisin Massacre marker. Though the marker is close to the battlefield, it is safest to drive through the intersection of North Dixie Highway and up East Elm Ave. as it is a busy intersection with no sidewalk. Find parking and make your way back to the intersection. The marker is on the north corner.

D Visit the site where American forces crossed the frozen river to engage the British. (*GPS – 1233 East Front St. Monroe, MI*) Return to the Dixie Highway intersection and take a right, crossing the river. Take the first left on East Front St. and look for the park on the left. A plaque commemorating the site stands beside the bridge to Sterling Island. Make your way across where you can see the River Raisin battlefield.

E Finish your tour of Monroe at the the Kentucky Soldiers Monument. (*GPS – 585 South Monroe St. Monroe, MI*) Head north on East Front St. until it intersects with South Monroe St. and then turn left. At the corner of West 7th St. and South Monroe you will see the memorial. Located in a small park, the monument  is dedicated to the victims of the River Raisin Massacre. A plaque describes how the location was the original graveyard of unidentified victims, and relates its transformation into a public park in 1904. The Kentucky Militia were stationed in the village of Frenchtown and successfully resisted British attacks until ordered to withdraw. Their determination to hold onto the town is also commemorated in Frankfort, Kentucky.

The Kentucky Soldier's Monument is sitting on the grounds of the former graveyard dedicated to the unknown victims of the River Raisin Massacre. [Nick Lachance]

Perrysburg & Fallen Timbers

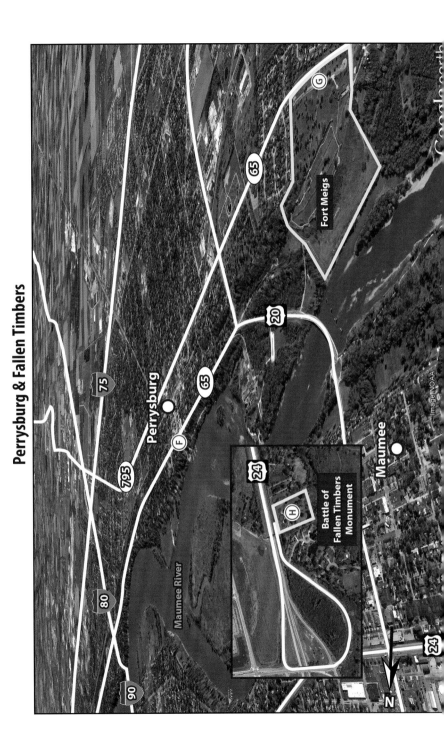

(F) After the River Raisin, continue on to Perrysburg, Ohio and Fort Meigs by returning to the I-75 South and continue until Exit 193 for US-20 South to Perrysburg. The city, named after the famous War of 1812 American Commodore Oliver Hazard Perry, offers a wider variety of hotels and restaurants than Monroe. Your first stop in downtown Perrysburg should be the statue of Commodore Perry located at the end of Louisiana Ave. (*GPS – 84 Louisiana Ave. Perrysburg, OH*) Overlooking the Maumee River, the statue and its location reflect the dreams of Perrysburg's founders and their hope of establishing a "New Orleans" of the north just a few kilometres up river from Lake Erie. Perrysburg has grown since then, but not nearly as much as its original residents had once hoped.

The monument in honour of Commodore Perry in Hood Park. [Nick Lachance]

A view inside the reconstruction of Fort Meigs. [Nick Lachance]

(G) A couple of kilometres to the southwest, along the Maumee River, stands Fort Meigs. (*GPS – 29100 West River Rd. (S.R. 65) Perrysburg, OH*) The Fort was reconstructed by the Ohio Historical Society in the late 1960s, and has been open to the public since 1974. Today it includes many structures built after the War of 1812, but you can still understand the value of its impressive fortifications and the difficulty the British had trying to take it in 1813. Staff at the visitor centre and inside the fort, are helpful and information panels explain the fort's initial and ongoing construction as well as the battle to defend it. On the flat plains outside of the Fort was where the British and First Nations soldiers failed to bait the American defenders out into open battle. Unable to take the fortification without heavier guns, they were forced to withdraw. For more information see fortmeigs.org.

(H) The monument at Fallen Timbers is not to be missed. (*GPS – 5643 State Park Rd. Maumee, OH*) It can be difficult to find without help. From the Fort Meigs parking lot, turn left on West Indiana Ave., then left again on West Boundary St. From there, turn left on OH-25 N/US-20 W/Maumee Reserve Rd., then left onto Highway 24-West. Take the exit toward Jerome Rd/Stitt Rd, and turn left immediately after the highway off ramp away from the mall onto Co Rd 2089 / Fallen Timbers Lane. Continue along Fallen Timbers Lane until the State Park appears on your right.

The Fallen Timbers State Memorial is worth the journey and one of the most interesting historical sites you will visit on this tour. In a well manicured lawn sits a grove of trees and three memorial sites: one for fallen the First Nations warriors, one for the American soldiers killed and wounded, and another commemorating the battle itself. Each represents a different memory

Tour

American militia defend during a re-enactment of the first siege of Fort Meigs. [Nick Lachance]

of the event. Here, more than any other memorial site you will visit on this tour, you can see the conflicting memory of the North American battlefields. The Battle of Fallen Timbers monument, erected in 1962, depicts General Anthony Wayne, the American commander, a Kentucky militiaman, and a First Nations warrior. All three of them look out to the horizon together, emphasizing the point that the battle was the beginning of a unified history for the two peoples. The monument to the American killed and wounded is far older, and was the first monument at this location. It has no mention of the First Nations warriors. Meanwhile, the memorial to the First Nations tribes that fought at Fallen Timbers was constructed in 1994, and equally does not mention the American soldiers. Each of the three represents a different memory of the battle and the aftermath.

The three monuments at Fallen Timbers. [Nick Lachance]

Tour

Touring the Upper St. Lawrence

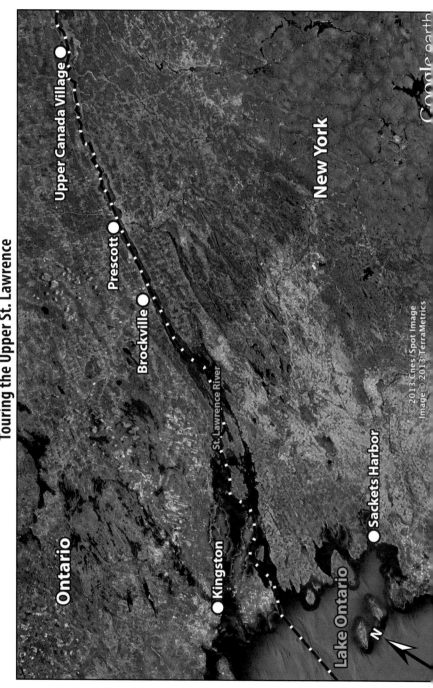

Touring the Upper St. Lawrence

Your tour of the upper Saint Lawrence River will take you from Eastern Ontario and across to the United States. The main points of interest are located in Kingston, Ontario and Sackets Harbor, New York. Kingston is situated midway between Toronto and Montréal and has a longtime history as a military and economic base due to its location near an international border crossing and transportation channel. The city became an important Great Lakes port in the 1830s upon the completion of the Rideau Canal. Rapid growth ensued and Kingston was designated the first capital of the Province of Canada in 1841.

Today the city's major educational institutions and tourist attractions heavily reflect its military history. With twenty-one National Historic Sites, Kingston has the third highest in Canada behind Ottawa and Toronto. Like Kingston, Sackets Harbor's strategic location made it a major shipbuilding and military installation throughout the 19th century. The Navy Shipyard was built during the War of 1812 and remained an active station until 1955. The site is located in the Sackets Harbor Village Historic District, a National Historic Place that is the source of much of the village's heritage and summer tourism.

The Martello Tower in the Kingston Harbour. [Benson Kua]

Tour

Morrisburg, Prescott & Brockville

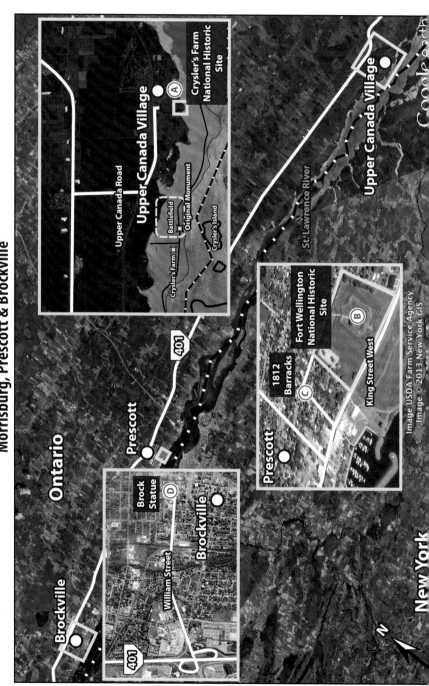

Morrisburg, Prescott & Brockville

(A) First on your tour is the Crysler's Farm memorial adjacent to Upper Canada village in Morrisburg. (*GPS – Upper Canada Village Heritage Park, 13740 County Rd. 2. Morrisburg, ON*) If westbound on the 401, take Exit 770 (Dickinson Dr.) south to County Rd. 2 and travel west. If eastbound take Exits 750 or 758 and travel south to County Rd. 2, then east on the county road. You can follow the routes of the two armies by exiting the 401 at Gananoque and continuing your journey east on the 1000 Islands Pwky. and County Rd. 2. Watch for signs for "Crysler's Farm Battlefield – 1813" or "Historical Plaque Crysler's Farm 1813." Turn into Upper Canada Village (the sign with the cannon) and you will see the monument on the horizon past the parking lot. Before heading out to the park, be sure to stop in at the visitors centre (Battlefield Memorial Building) which houses a mural of the battle, an audio-visual presentation, and some artefacts.

The original Crysler's Farm battlefield was designated a National Historic Site in 1920 and boasted a large granite monument erected by the Dominion government in 1895. The majority of John Crysler's farm area was flooded when the St. Lawrence Seaway was constructed in 1958, so a new site was established on the river beside Upper Canada Village. The granite obelisk was relocated to this new site and placed atop a mound, made from earth removed from the original site, at the south end of Crysler Park. It is flanked by a pair of 24-pounder cannons.

1940s postcard of the monument at Crysler's Farm. [Photogelatine Engravings Co.]

B Stop next at the Fort Wellington National Historic Site, located at the corner of King St. East (Highway #2) and VanKoughnet St. in Prescott, Ontario. (*GPS – Fort Wellington National Historic Site, 370 Vankoughnet St. Prescott, Ontario*) The fort was established during the War of 1812 as both a communications post and deterrent to defend the shipping route along the St. Lawrence River. Two 24-pounder guns with the range to reach the American shore at Ogdensburg protected the bateaux transhipping goods over the rapids. The structure was mainly earth ramparts with a vertical timber palisade and was never attacked during the war. The fort did see action in 1813 when General Wilkinson's flotilla reached Prescott during an attempt to capture Montréal. The American boats, less the soldiers who had disembarked to stay out of harm's way, crept through the town during the night. The two armies went on to fight the Battle of Crysler's Farm.

Fort Wellington is one of the best preserved nineteenth-century fortifications in Canada. Originally built in 1838-39, the fort was acquired by the Historic Sites and Monuments Board in 1924 in extremely good condition. The site opened as a heritage site only one year later, and has since been rebuilt to appear as it did in the 1846 when it served as one of the many posts ready to defend the not-so undefended border.

You will begin your visit at the new visitor centre and then follow the path through the site. Exhibitions in the visitor centre focus on the role of the local militia, British military, and First Nations in protecting the St. Lawrence River, Prescott, and British supply lines during the War of 1812.

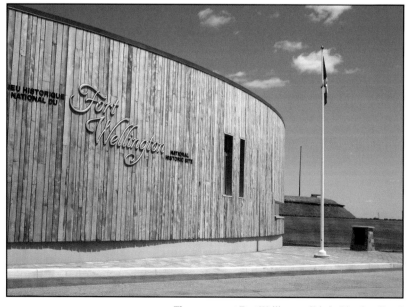

The museum at Fort Wellington. [Linda Risacher Copp]

Fort Wellington. [Dennis Jarvis]

The highlight is an 1812 era British gunboat that is 18 metres long and five metres wide, was recovered from the river by Parks Canada underwater archaeologists near Mallorytown and moved to Fort Wellington.

Dry ditches and a 2.8 metre high wooden stakewall surround the fort. Within this line of defence are earth ramparts with posts projecting outwards to discourage an enemy's effort to scale the walls. The main gate is the only entrance to the fort and is situated in the north wall because an attack was likely to come from the direction of the river. Inside the fort you will find timber buildings of the officer's quarters, latrine, and blockhouse which contain the gunpowder magazine and barracks. Only two original buildings are missing: the guardhouse, to the east of the main gates, and the cookhouse, between the officer's quarters and the latrine. From inside the fort, visitors will appreciate the value of the site viewing Ogdensburg and the American shore a short distance across the river.

Fort Wellington is open from May until October. Entrance fees are modest in the off-season and increase slightly during the summer months. Parents and grandparents might wish to be forewarned that the fort encourages young children to play with toy muskets, showing them how soldiers lined up to fire volleys at each other.

Note that there are two Historic Sites and Monuments Board plaques located on the site. The first, which offers an overview of the history of the fort, is near the visitor centre at King St. The second outlines the role of the fort during the War of 1812 and is on the third floor of the blockhouse on a wall between panels "A Military Depot" and "A New Mandate."

Tour

Undated Postcard of the Prescott Barracks.

C If you would like to see more sites related to Fort Wellington, take a short walk to see the building that housed a barracks during the War of 1812. From the fort turn right on VanKoughnet St. left on Dibble St. and left until 356 East St. The stone house was part of the Prescott garrison and functioned as a barracks for militiamen and British regulars until 1815 when a hospital was added to the second floor. The structure is one of the oldest surviving military buildings in Ontario. Its exterior has been restored to how it looked in the early 19th century and the original interior design has been well preserved. Look for a stone Historic Sites marker on its right side.

A plaque describing the Capture of Ogdensburg in 1813 is also within walking range, in a park at the foot of Sophia St. at the western edge of Prescott. Prescott is an interesting town that hosts the remarkable St. Lawrence Shakespeare festival with comedy performances inspired by Shakespearian plays. Downstream from Prescott but within sight of the town is the 60-foot tall stone windmill that became the focus of the Battle of the Windmill, a skirmish fought with supporters of the Rebellions of 1837-38. Nearby there is the Heritage Waterfront Trail that offers great views of the river. If you have time stop at the popular Red George Public House, a restaurant named after Lieutenant-Colonel Macdonell "Red George" who commanded the Glengarry Fencibles and led them in the capture of Ogdensburg.

D On your way to Kingston, you may wish to stop in Brockville to view the statue of the city's namesake, General Isaac Brock. *(GPS – 41 Court House Square. Brockville, ON)* The naming of the city in 1812 was a citizen-led movement inspired in part by Brock's recent success in securing the surrender of Fort Detroit. He was never able to formally accept the honour before his death. A bust of Brock sits atop a granite pillar outside the courthouse downtown.

Nearby is a plaque describing Major Benjamin Forsyth's raid on Brockville in February 1813. With a detachment of 200 men, Forsyth crossed the St. Lawrence River from Morristown, N.Y. and attacked Brockville. The local militia was taken completely by surprised and the invaders were able to release prisoners from the jail, steal quantity of arms, horses and cattle, and even kidnapped some residents. The resentment aroused by this raid led to the successful British attack on Ogdensburg, New York. The plaque is located at the foot of Apple St. south of Water St. West.

To learn more about how important control of the St. Lawrence was, you may also wish to view a Historic Sites plaque describing the 1814 defences on Chimney Island. The island became a refuge for British gunboats when a blockhouse and 18-pounder canon were placed on the site. The plaque is located opposite the island on the Thousand Islands Pwky. 2.3km east of Mallorytown Rd.

Brock's bust outside the courthouse in Brockville. [City of Brockville]

Tour

Kingston

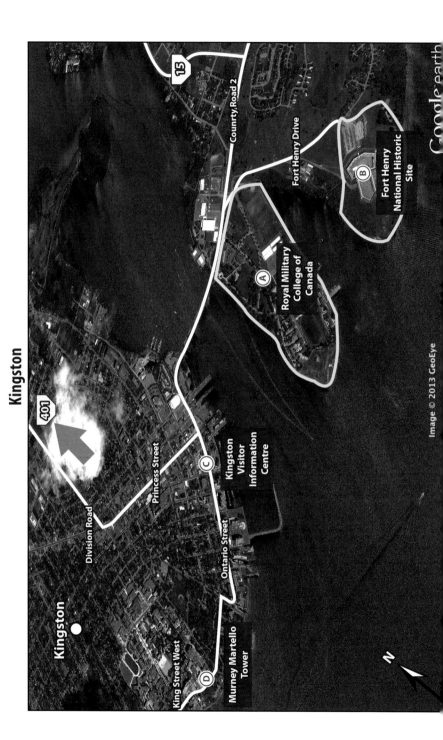

Image © 2013 GeoEye

Google earth

15

County Road 2

Fort Henry Drive

B Fort Henry National Historic Site

A Royal Military College of Canada

401

Kingston

Division Road

Princess Street

C Kingston Visitor Information Centre

Ontario Street

King Street West

D Murney Martello Tower

N

Kingston

Kingston, the naval base for the Provincial Marine and then the Royal Navy, played a major role in the War of 1812. The dockyard where most of the ships of Commodore Yeo's Squadron were built, including HMS *St. Lawrence,* was guarded by earthen ramparts with canon on Point Frederick and a similar position across the bay at Point Henry. Six wooden blockhouses ringed the harbour providing additional protection. Despite its obvious strategic importance, Kingston was never seriously attacked during the War of 1812 though the guns of Fort Frederick fired on the American fleet during the *Royal George* incident in November 1812.

After the war ended, Kingston became one of the most important defensive positions developed to deter or defeat a future American invasion. Fort Frederick became the main fortification and after 1840 four large Martello Towers were constructed to replace the blockhouses. During the 1846 Oregon crisis, the fort's earth walls were added to further protect the Martello Tower. In 1852 the dockyard was closed and the fort was abandoned in 1870.

Visitors flock to Kingston and its military sites during the summer months. On your tour you will visit sites across the city, beginning at Fort Frederick and Fort Henry on the grounds of Royal Military College and ending in downtown Kingston at the Murney Martello Tower and Museum.

(A) Your tour of Point (Fort) Frederick will take you around the peninsula of the Royal Military College of Canada via Point Frederick Dr. *(GPS – Royal Military College of Canada, General Crerar Cres. Kingston, ON)* As you enter the grounds on Valour Dr., note the right stone gate post whose outward facing side boasts a plaque to Sir James Lucas Yeo, the successful British naval commander who is known for defending Sackets Harbor and capturing Oswego in 1814. On the opposite post is a plaque offering the history of Point Frederick and the surviving buildings that comprised the old naval base.

Continue on Point Frederick Dr. One of the four Martello towers is still standing near the southern end and is easy to spot by its bulbous base and red roof. Next to the structure is a plaque describing the role these towers played in the defence of the post. From here, follow the road just past the Parade Square until Valour Dr. and stop in front of the Stone Frigate. To the left of the main door a plaque marks the former Kingston Navy Yard, established in 1789. The dockyard was guarded by earthen ramparts with canons at the ready on Point Frederick. Here is where most of Commodore Yeo's Squadron ships were built.

(B) Fort Henry sits atop Point Henry on the adjacent peninsula. *(GPS – Fort Henry National Historic Site, 1 Fort Henry Dr. Kingston,*

A view of Fort Frederick from Fort Henry. [Dennis Jarvis]

ON) From the navy yard go north on General Crerar Cres., turn right on Precision Dr., and right on Fort Henry Dr. Stop next to the tourist kiosk to view the Fort Henry monument, an anchor and pillar erected in honour of those who served on Lake Ontario during the War of 1812. Take the right fork and arrive at the entrance to Fort Henry National Historic Site. Note the plaque mounted on the wall to the right of the door which offers a concise history of the fort.

The original Fort Henry was built during the War of 1812, but it was replaced by this modern structure in 1836 to increase defence of the Rideau Canal. The Ontario Department of Highways began restoration of the site in 1936 in an effort to boost tourism in the region. After some landscaping and masonry repairs, preservation of the site became the paramount goal and work expanded to include refurbishing interior spaces and furnishings. The fort opened to the public in 1938 as a well-dressed and functioning heritage site. In 2012, the fort unveiled a 10,000 square foot Discovery Centre located beyond the parking lot. Inside are interactive exhibits, a gift shop, and a café. From this vantage point you can also enjoy breathtaking panoramic views of the coast.

The fort is comprised of an upper fort and a lower fort. The upper fort contains most of the administration rooms and washrooms, while more than ten different rooms in the lower fort have been restored to allow visitors to get a sense of their military usage. A complete list of the many rooms inside the fort is available on their website, though highlights include the soldier's barracks, bakery, garrison cells, and magazine. Each room has been restored and is dressed to look as it would have in the fort's prime. Exhibits and artefacts increase the authenticity of the site.

The fort runs on a daily series of educational programs and events which will entertain both children and adults. A daily schedule is available on their website if you wish to pre-plan your trip. During your visit you are guaranteed to see a demonstration put on by the Fort Henry Guard, and volunteers in civilian clothing dressed as schoolteachers and soldiers wives. Haunted Walks of Kingston conducts year-round night tours of the Fort. If interested, you can also view Fort Henry from Cartwright Point, accessible by taking Lundy's Lane. to Dieppe Ave. and through to the end of the Point Rd.

C From Fort Henry, take the bridge across the water into downtown Kingston, following Ontario St. until just before Clarence St. *(GPS – Kingston Visitor Information Centre, 209 Ontario St. Kingston, ON)* Pull into the Visitor Centre parking lot and walk towards the water. On a stone wall sits two plaques describes the Kingston fortifications during the War of 1812 and marks the site of the vital Royal Naval Dockyard. This location is part of the Waterfront Pathway and it links up with the next site, so you can easily walk or bike there if you choose to leave your car here.

D Your final stop will be the Murney Martello Tower on the waterfront which contains a museum focusing on military life in the 19th century. *(GPS – Murney Tower National Historic Site, 18 King St. West. Kingston, ON)* The tower is located at Murney Point in MacDonald Park and, like its counterpart located at Point Frederick, is easy to spot because of its red roof. Unlike the one at Point Frederick, though, this tower was not built until 1849. The tower is a National Historic Site managed by the Kingston Historical Society. A plaque rests on a pillar near the entrance. The museum is open during the summer months and displays include uniforms, artillery, and military artefacts.

The Murney Martello Tower museum. [Dennis Jarvis]

Sackets Harbor

Crossing the Border: Sackets Harbor

Following the outbreak of war in June 1812, Sackets Harbor became the centre of American military and naval activity for Lake Ontario and the St. Lawrence Valley. The village saw action on 29 May 1813 when a combination of British regular and colonial militia attempted to destroy the American shipyard. Though the Americans defended the Harbor, a fire destroyed their military stores. Sackets Harbor remained an active naval station throughout the war and its dockyard facilities were maintained by the navy until 1955.

One way to visit Sackets Harbor, the American Châteauguay naval base during the War of 1812, is to take the ferry from Kingston to Wolfe Island. The pleasant and free 20 minute journey allows you to view Kingston Harbour and Fort Henry. Follow Highway 95 to the south end of the island, ignoring or admiring the numerous wind turbines, and embark on Horne's ferry, a privately owned first come-first served service to Cape Vincent in New York state. Information on both ferries may be found at wolfeisland.com/ferry. Cape Vincent itself is a pleasant village. Alternatively, the Ogdensburg bridge and the 1000 Island International Bridge is open year round and the trip along the river to Alexandria Bay is stunning.

The trip takes ten minutes and the formalities of entry into the United States are effectively dealt with at Cape Vincent. The drive to Sackets Harbor is about 40 minutes. It is evident that the village takes pride in its history. Anyone with an interest in the naval encounters of 1812-14 will find much to see here. The yacht-filled harbor and battlefield historic site are at the western end of the attractive village. It is possible to retrace the route the British and Canadian troops followed from Horse Island to the edge of the Harbor a distance of a little more than a kilometre.

Re-enactors at Sackets Harbor. [NYSOPRHP-BHS]

Sackets Harbor has a host of superb restaurants see sacketsharborny.com for more information. The chain hotels are in nearby Watertown but there are a number of high quality B & B's as well as the Ontario Place Hotel in the village (sacketsharborny.com/accomodations).

Before beginning your tour, be sure to stop by the Heritage Area Visitors' Center located in Market Square Park at West Main and Bayard Streets. The newly dedicated 1812 Bicentennial Peace Garden in the park is only a block away beside the Union Hotel building (1817).

(A) Begin your tour at the Sackets Harbor Battlefield State Site, once named "Old Battlefield Park." *(GPS – 504 West Main St. Sackets Harbor, NY)* Although the walk around the site is a short one, it allows you to explore the naval yard site and portions of the May 1813 battlefield. It also offers panoramic views of Lake Ontario.

In 1812, Fort Tompkins was hastily constructed on the grounds where the Commandants house now stands (1847) and the navy yard, which is marked by an American flag rising above the private navy point marina complex. The fort's structures consisted of a blockhouse, earthworks, and artillery pieces. Nearby, a barracks containing the southwest Basswood (Smith) Cantonment Blockhouse (1813) housed soldiers. After the Second Battle of Sackets Harbor, a palisade and earthworks named Fort Kentucky was constructed to strengthen the defences. In 1860, all of the earthen fortifications were levelled and became farmland while the structures were either demolished or converted for agricultural use.

In 1913, in honour of the centennial of the War of 1812, a small portion of the battlefield called "The Old Battle Ground" was officially recognized as

The dedication of the monument at Sackets Harbor by then Assistant Secretary of the Navy Franlkin D. Roosevelt (left), 29 May 1913. [NYSOPRHP-BHS]

Re-enactors at Sackets Harbor Battlefield State Park. [NYSOPRHP-BHS]

a site of remembrance. The site was renamed Centennial Park and a granite monument to the war dead was erected and surrounded by one hundred trees. Between 1967 and 1974, the State of New York acquired several parcels of land adjacent to the battlefield site, including Centennial Park, and began a program to make the area accessible to the public. In 1974 the Sackets Harbor Battlefield was listed on the National Register of Historic Places and the Sackets Harbor Historical Society formed as a local entity to promote interest in the site. Since then, New York State has taken an active role in acquiring more of the historic battlegrounds and continues to work to revitalize the area. There are 10 modern interpretative panels on the history trail, plus several other explanatory notes on the various canon's and directional battle maps to help explain the grounds.

The Sackets Habour Battlefield State Historic Site, Sackets Harbor Battlefield Alliance, and the Community of Sackets Harbor are working together on an initiative which will see a granite monument placed overlooking Black River Bay at the eastern end of Lake Ontario. This 'Memorial to the Crown Forces' will commemorate both the bicentennial and those who were killed at the Second Battle of Sackets Harbor. The Crown Forces buried in an unmarked grave will be honoured with each man's unit, name and rank engraved on a large granite ledger.

(B) A number of the forts that defended Sackets Harbor during the war existed outside of the boundaries of the modern State Site, but if you walk through the village you should be able to find markers indicating where they once stood. The Fort Virginia Blockhouse (1812-1815) was located at the current intersection of Ambrose and Washington Streets. The site of Fort

Tour

Chauncey, a stone tower, was located near the town's current fire station at Main and Broad Streets. The general site of Fort Stark lies on private land on the east side of Monroe St. south of Dodge Ave. The village of Sackets Harbor was once surrounded by a line of earthworks stretching from Fort Kentucky to Fort Pike (previously Fort Volunteer). The remaining portions of the earthen wall can be seen at the Fort Pike site in Madison Barracks.

The remains of Fort Kentucky, an earthen redoubt and a 32-pounder. [NYSOPRHP-BHS]

Ⓒ For those interested in military architecture, Madison Barracks is a great place to visit. (*GPS – 85 Worth Rd. Sackets Harbor, NY*) The first limestone structure was named after President James Madison and constructed between 1816 and 1819. It was an active American Army post from the War of 1812 to 1945 and many famous American leaders used it as temporary living quarters. Today, the buildings are part of the National Register of Historic Places and is considered "a living history museum of military architecture."

The military cemetery at Sackets Harbor. [Constance Barone]

D The burial ground for those killed during the War of 1812 is located in Madison Barracks. *(GPS – Sackets Harbor Military Cemetery, North Broad St. Sackets Harbor, NY)* The Madison Barracks Military Cemetery, established along Military Rd. was moved in 1909 to its present day location on Dodge Ave. The cemetery contains two relevant memorials related to the War of 1812. The first is the tombstone monument of Brigadier General Zebulon Pike, who was killed in 1813 during the explosion of the gunpower magazine at the Battle of York (present day Toronto). Adjacent to Pike's memorial is the Tomb of the Unknown Soldiers honouring those who were killed at the Battle of Sackets Harbor, buried on the grounds but do not have a known grave.

This undated postcard shows the Tomb of the Unknown Soldiers from the battle at Sackets Harbor. The monument was dedicated 31 May 1888 in Madison Barracks. The monument in the background commemorates the death of Brigadier General Zebulon Pike. Today, the two monuments sit in the same graveyard but the landscape is more sparse today than what you see in the postcard. [Robert & Jeanine Brennan, Town & Village Historians]

Touring the Upper Great Lakes Region

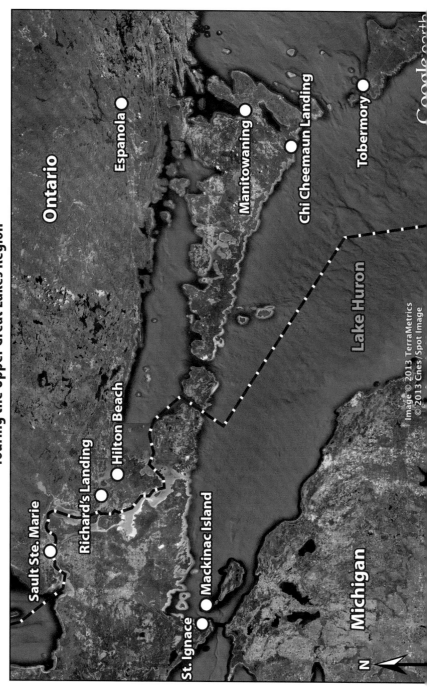

Touring the Upper Great Lakes Region

The Great Lakes are far enough away from the urban centres of southern Ontario and Michigan that much of the forested landscape remains like it was two centuries ago. Today the small towns that dot the shores of Lake Huron and Lake Superior are much easier to reach. In 1812 any long distance travel was done by boat through the country's rivers and lakes. The only other option to reach the Northwest frontier towns of Sault St Marie or St. Ignace was to walk, a task of months rather than the weeks-long boat journey. Now you can drive there while still enjoying the picturesque scenery of northern Ontario and Upper Michigan. In addition to the historic sites along your route, there are many hotels, bed and breakfasts and national parks where you can stop to enjoy the natural beauty of this tour.

The War of 1812 is better remembered in the places on this tour than in the larger cities where historic sites have been taken over by urban sprawl. The memory of their frontier past is still preserved in tourist offices and museums, and 1812 marks one of the few examples where their towns and forts became battlegrounds rather than part of the forgotten periphery of North America. As you drive around the Great Lakes, try to remember that these once disparate communities were only connected by boat and otherwise existed in isolation from their eastern compatriots. It was a very different sort of war on the frontier, but a war nonetheless.

Sunrise on Miller Lake, Tobermory, Ontario. [Zach Houston]

Manitowaning

Queen Street

Manitowaning

Assiginack Museum

Arthur Street

Meredith Street

Manitowaning Bay

© 2013 Cnes /Spot Image

Chi Cheemaun Ferry

St. Joseph Island & Mackinac

The Northwestern frontier of the War of 1812 stretches around Lake Huron from the fur-trading post at Sault Ste. Marie, to the British fort on St. Joseph Island, to the American fort at Mackinac Island. Today, these areas are tied together by a shared history of their frontier past and a common interest in encouraging tourists to visit this distant region of Ontario and Michigan. They are as much as a frontier to the urban centres of southern Ontario and Michigan as they were to the fur traders and colonists of Upper Canada and the American territories. The trip around Lake Huron is a long drive, but well worth it. More than any other tour, driving through the forests that surround the great lake allows you to "see the ground" as it once was and, more importantly, envision the distances and separation of frontier life. Outside of the small towns that dot your route, the road often stretches through an uninterrupted ocean of trees – an impassable barrier. No wonder all serious transportation occurred in the region's many waterways.

Where to begin this tour depends on where you are starting. If you are located in eastern or northern Ontario, you can take 400 Highway to Highway 69 and approach Sault Ste. Marie via Sudbury. If you have the time, make your way to Tobermory on the tip of the Bruce Peninsula which separates Lake Huron from Georgian Bay. From Tobermory you can catch the Chi Cheemaun Ferry (ontarioferries.com) which travels to Manitoulin Island. Although it is a longer trip than simply driving around Georgian Bay, the scenic route is breathtaking and the leisurely cruise across to the island is far more relaxing. Whichever route you choose, it is a long drive.

(A) If you take the Chi Cheemaun to Manitoulin Island, the small village of Manitowaning is worth a visit on your way north. The Assiginack Museum holds many artefacts from the island's former residents. Their excellent collection ranges from 19th century pottery and glassware to items brought back from Canada's wars. As you leave the village, there is a monument to Jesuit missionaries with a lookout point offering a stunning view across the island.

Driving north from Manitowaning following Highway 6, you will eventually cross through Espanola and then connect back with the Trans-Canada, Highway 17. Espanola is the largest city you will pass through until Sault Ste. Marie, so you may wish to stop there for lunch. Otherwise, press on to reach St. Joseph Island by sundown! As you drive along the shore, you are also following the route of *voyageurs* from the fur trade who would have followed the Ottawa River to Lake Nipissing to Georgian Bay from Montréal. They too may have stopped at Fort St. Joseph or continued to Sault Ste. Marie.

(B) There are two major villages on St Joseph Island, Richard's Landing and Hilton Beach. Both are small, quiet places worth spending a

St. Joseph's Island

relaxing night watching the waters of the North Channel. There are two important sites you should visit while on the island. The first is Parks Canada National Historic Site, Fort St. Joseph on the southern most tip of the island. Like most of the island, the fort is surrounded by peaceful forests. The visitor's centre and small exhibit room as well as the remains of the fort are worth exploring.

The occupants of Fort St. Joseph's once described their posting "military Siberia," but it is far more hospitable today. The exhibits at Fort St. Joseph depict life there in 1812 and explain its construction and role in the War of 1812. They focus on the experience of soldiers and merchants who would have stayed at the Fort in the early 19th century and the hardships they endured. There are furs, muskets, and a reconstruction of a merchant's cabin. As usual, Parks Canada has excellent informational panels.

Once you are done in the exhibit room, walk down a short path through the forest to see the fort's ruins. Fort St. Joseph was burned by attacking Americans forces who found it abandoned – its soldiers having all gone to attack and occupy Fort Mackinac to the south. After the war, the British chose not to rebuild and instead built a new fort on Drummond Island, between St. Joseph and Mackinaw. All that remains today is the crumbling, aged stone outline of long collapsed buildings. Ropes have been placed to demark the old buildings' boundaries.

While walking the grounds of the old fort, note where the tree line begins, not necessarily what has been mowed by the park's staff. That is the boundary of the old fort, where each tree was laboriously removed and stumps cleared from the ground. Imagine it in 1812, when that forest and the

The display at Fort St. Joseph. [Nick Lachance]

A diorama gives visitors an impression of Fort St. Joseph. [Nick Lachance]

water stretching out before you would have been the boundary of the world for those stationed at the fort. To your southeast is Drummond Island, where Fort St. Joseph's successor was built. The invading force of British soldiers and First Nations warriors that attacked Mackinac Island would have disappeared over that southern horizon through the East Channel between Drummond Island and Upper Michigan. The Hilton Beach Inn, named after the beach, not the hotel chain, and the Clansman Motel are recommended.

(C) Before you leave for Sault Ste. Marie it is worth stopping briefly at St. Joseph Island Museum on the way. Located on the corner of I Line and 20th Sideroad, the museum is spread over several different buildings. Much like the museum in Manitowaning, it will give you a taste of the local island history.

Farming equipment used by locals displayed in the local island museum. [Nick Lachance]

A view of Ermatinger House. [Nick Lachance]

D From St. Joseph Island, return north along Highway 548 and connect with the Trans Canada Highway to Sault Ste. Marie. One site worth visiting is the Ermatinger House, the oldest stone structure in Northwest Ontario and home of Sault Ste. Marie's major independent trader, Charles Oakes Ermatinger located at 831 Queen St. East. Ermatinger was a trader during the War of 1812 and a significant figure for the frontier fur trade. The house, like many of the stops on this tour, offers a glimpse into the life on the frontier and a very different world from the Canadians of 1812 to the south. You may also wish to stop at the Clergue Blockhouse next door, though a more recent structure, is also linked to the fur trade.

Sault Ste. Marie

St. Ignace on the south tip of Upper Michigan across from Mackinac Island is a short hour long drive away. You will again travel through long stretches of forest, unchanged from the frontier of two centuries past. St. Ignace has a wide range of affordable hotels where you may choose to stay, most of them facing the waters of Lake Huron. If you can afford some luxury there are upscale hotels on Mackinac Island. Visit mackinac.com for details.

Ferry services operate out of St. Ignace to Mackinac Island, which has been transformed from its origins as an isolated trading outpost. It is now a tourist hotspot and no cars are allowed on the island but visitors can tour it by bicycle or by horse drawn carriages (or snowmobile in the winter). As you arrive by ferry, you can catch a glimpse of the houses on the island, ranging from rustic to palatial. Historic Fort Mackinac is here, but it is well worth your time visiting other attractions on the island as well.

No cars are allowed on beautiful Mackinac Island. [Nick Lachance]

(E) Upon docking at the harbour, Fort Mackinac is a short walk. It rests upon a cliff overlooking the bay and at its base is a statue of Jacques Marquette, the Jesuit missionary who founded St. Ignace. While few of the buildings in the fort were originally there in 1812, the commanding view of the water points to the fort's important location for the region. As you are touring, make sure to spend some time examining the back of the fort that faces inland. It was here where British soldiers, landing on the north side of the island, attacked the fort and successfully forced its surrender.

(F) If you have time visit the rest of the island and take in the battlefield site of 1814, when American soldiers attempted to retake Fort Mackinac. The island is known for its fudge and ice cream shops (during the summer at least) and many other stores for the tourists visiting.

(G) Those with a keen interest in the war may want to take a short walk or take a carriage ride along Garrison Rd. to the Fort Mackinac Post Cemetery. The sombre final resting place of more than 100 American soldiers

Fort Mackinac. [Nick Lachance]

is one of only four cemeteries, along with Arlington, Gettysburg, and the Punchbowl, that always fly their flags at half-mast.

St. Ignace and Mackinac Island are a long drive for only a few sites related to the War of 1812, but it is a wonderful vacation spot for a family or a couple. If you have the money, we recommend staying a few days in the area and exploring the island and taking in the sights of Upper Michigan. You can experience the 1812 frontier atmosphere of vast untouched forests and some modern day amenities.

Mackinac Island

Touring Toronto, Hamilton & the Niagara Region

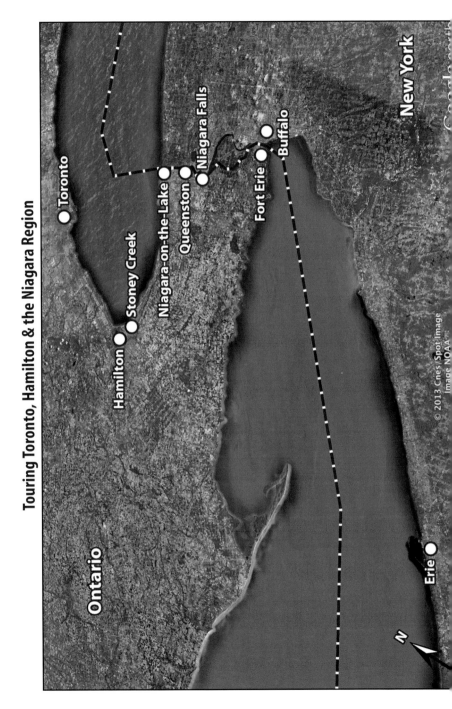

Ontario

Toronto

Hamilton

Stoney Creek

Niagara-on-the-Lake

Queenston

Niagara Falls

Fort Erie

Buffalo

New York

Erie

N

© 2013 Cnes / Spot Image
Image NOAA

Touring Toronto, Hamilton & the Niagara Region

This tour skirts around Ontario's tourist centre and there are many places you may wish to visit outside of historical sites. In 1793, Toronto, then known as York, was recognized as the capital of the new colony of Upper Canada. The city was renamed Toronto in 1834 and grew as a centre for railways and shipping. In the late 19th century, under the business acumen of Joseph Flavelle, Toronto emerged as the financial capital of Canada. After the Second World War, many of Canada's new immigrants chose to settle in the area causing a population boom that made it the largest city in Canada. Toronto quickly became a global city and remains the business and financial capital of Canada. It is internationally renowned for its performing arts, nightlife, and various eclectic districts. Downtown Toronto is one of the largest urban centres in North America and is the location of the Eaton Centre, Canada's fourth largest shopping centre with over 330 stores and over one million visitors a week. Other notable attractions include the Royal Ontario Museum, Hockey Hall of Fame, Air Canada Centre, and the distinctive CN Tower.

Toronto and Hamilton, located in the centre of the Golden Horseshoe subregion, have two of the largest seaports in Lake Ontario. Hamilton's is the busiest in all the Great Lakes with most of the cargo enabling it to function as the largest steel manufacturing city in Canada. Hamilton is located on the western end of the Niagara Peninsula and the Niagara Escarpment runs through the middle of the city horizontally, separating the city into upper and lower parts. Attractions in the Hamilton region include the Canadian Warplane Heritage Museum, Royal Botanical Gardens, African Lion Safari, the Art Gallery of Hamilton, and the Canadian Football Hall of Fame.

Nearby, the Niagara region holds one of Ontario's greatest natural phenomena, the Niagara Falls. The Falls straddle the American and Canadian border and are just a few kilometres south of some of the sites you will visit on this tour. The Falls were one of Canada's first major tourist attractions, becoming internationally recognized as a honeymoon location for travellers from around the world. The Niagara Peninsula is also the site of many of the provinces fine wineries. Stretching across the land south of Lake Ontario, you might also choose to stop at some Niagara wineries on this tour. Niagara-on-the-Lake, north of Niagara, Ontario, is a charming base to visit the wine region – and if you are travelling in the summer, the site of the Shaw Festival where the plays of George Bernard Shaw are celebrated.

Tour

Tour

Toronto

Don Valley Parkway

1812 Interpretation Centre

(G)

Toronto

Toronto Island

Bathurst Street

Monument to The War of 1812

(D)

Bathurst Street

Victoria Square

(C)

Fort York

(A)

(B)

Fleet Street

Coronation Park

(E)

Burial Grounds

Defence of York Plaque

(F)

Lake Shore Boulevard West

Gardiner Expressway

N

Toronto

York has grown from a small waterside village in the early 1800s to the most populous and financially powerful metropolis in Canada. It is the most extreme example of the social, culture and economic growth in North America over the past 200 years. It is also home to the largest collection of original War of 1812 buildings. The tour of the Toronto sites to the War of 1812 will take you through the west side of the city's downtown core.

Fort York was an isolated outpost located on the shore on Lake Ontario and to the east of York (Toronto), a village of roughly 800 residents. About 400 regulars and a small number of militiamen lived in the fort. On 27 April 1813, Fort York was attacked by American forces and the city occupied, pillaged, and then partially burned down. Outnumbered and forced to retreat eastward, British commander Major-General Sir Roger Sheaffe made his infamous decision to blow up the fort's gunpower magazine containing up to 300 pounds of black powder and hundreds of cannon and musket balls. The blast, which projected out of the magazine doorway approximately 50km to the west, caused heavy American casualties and struck down General Zebluon Pike. The Americans eventually retreated, and Fort York remained a military outpost until the beginning of the 20th century.

Driving is an option but be warned Toronto is the most congested city in Canada. However you choose to get downtown, the harbour front is much nicer on foot or on bicycle. Cycling is popular in the city and bikes can be rented from Toronto's public bike sharing system, Bixi, which has over 50 stations throughout the city (toronto.bixi.com). The Toronto Transit Commission (TTC.ca) is convenient and the routes run often.

The modern buildings that surround Fort York. [Caitlin McWilliams]

Tour

(A) Fort York exists today as a historic site of military fortifications and related buildings and exhibits. (*GPS – 100 Garrison Rd. Toronto, ON*) Take the Gardiner Expressway downtown and exit at Lake Shore Blvd. / Jameson Ave. Turn left at Stratchan Ave., right onto Fleet St., and left on Garrison Rd., which will take you around a bend to the parking lot and the West Gate entrance. Fort York is uniquely located in the heart of the major metropolis. Despite being surrounded on all sides by highrises and highways, the fort's walls create enough of a barrier to immerse yourself in the historical context of the War of 1812. The mere fact that the fortification stands today, despite the centuries of redevelopment in Toronto's city core, is a testament to its value as a site of local history and of the greater legacy of the war as a whole.

Fort York was completely rebuilt, purchased by the city of Toronto in 1909, and opened as a public museum in 1934. Since then it has undergone different levels of restoration and today the fort remains with about half of the buildings that existed in the 1930s. Eight of these buildings are some of the oldest in Toronto. Though more structures existed during the war, they were destroyed when the magazine exploded during the American occupation in 1813. No evidence of these lost buildings remains on the surface; however, you can see a variety of what else has been unearthed in the Blue Barracks exhibits. The highlight includes bits of debris thrown outwards when the magazine exploded, including pieces of twisted steel and charred timber found under the parking lot. Archaeologists have also recently discovered the site of the former Government House, the first official residence of the Lieutenant-Governor of Upper Canada. Burned bits of timber and brick similar to that in site plans suggest that the one-storey, U-shaped building originally stood in the centre of the fort. An informative panel marks the spot where Government House once stood on the right side of the fort just past the first barracks.

The 45-minute guided tour is highly recommended. A friendly volunteer in time-period garb will take you through a number of the original structures. The insight, offered by the guides, on how the landscape has changed is invaluable. Remember that the fort originally stood at the shoreline which has shifted over the last two centuries. A look over the north wall down into the train tracks gives you a sense of the fort's original 30-foot natural embankment. The ramparts that surround the fort are original. The sunken ground next to the blockhouse shows you the original elevation of the ground inside. A diorama of Toronto circa 1817 located in the blockhouse is helpful for visualizing the drastic geographical change of the region.

Not only is the fort's landscape and exterior impressive, but the gems contained within its walls – the authentic structures, archival displays, and hourly demonstrations – combine to make the tour a tangible, educational,

Tour

186

and authentic experience. The exhibits show artefacts and use multi-lingual panels to effectively contextualize the displays within the greater themes of the war. It is evident that the curators have worked to present a well-rounded view of the war by exploring the British, American, Natives, and civilian experience. Exhibits geared towards children are either computer-enhanced or hands-on. In the kitchen, costumed guides prepare dishes made from ingredients and methods used during the early 1800s and the samples are an experience in and of itself. Rooms are staged to look as they did in their prime. Be sure to stay long enough to see the impressive firing display using either firearms or cannons put on every hour by the Fort York Guard.

The firing display at Fort York. [Caitlin McWilliams]

(B) After touring Fort York, walk the short distance to the western edge of the Garrison Commons to the Strachan Ave. Burial Ground. The Strachan Ave. Burial Ground was the city's third military cemetery and is the final resting place for about 150 soldiers and family members associated with the fort. In 1970, after a long period of dilapidation, Parks Canada collected the remaining tablets and mounted them in the brick wall. The majority of the headstones have experienced extreme weathering and are unreadable, and since the cemetery records are incomplete, many cannot be identified. The city of Toronto has plans to turn part of this area into a visitor's centre as part of its Fort York revitalization project.

(C) Stop next at Victoria Square Memorial Park, the site of Toronto's first military cemetery. (*GPS – 10 Niagara St, Toronto, ON*) The park is only a five minute drive from the fort but there is no parking lot, so you may

Tour

choose to walk the 10 minutes instead. Exit onto Fort York Blvd., turn left on Bathurst St. right at Niagara St. and the park will be on your right as you approach Portland St.

Toronto's first military cemetery is the burial site of more than 400 men, women, children, and horses connected with the fort who died between 1793 and 1863. Individuals associated with Fort York were first buried here before being moved elsewhere. The site became a public park at the turn of the 19th century but experienced bouts of vandalism, grave robbing, and neglect. Similar to the site at Stratchan Ave., the seventeen weathered headstones on display on the east side of the park are all that remain, but here they are labelled because city records exist. The perimeter of the park is marked by placards describing the history of the site. The centrepiece of the park is the monument to the War of 1812 sculpted in 1907 by Toronto native Walter Seymour Allward. Allward is most famous for designing the Canadian National Vimy Memorial in France. The monument in Toronto depicts an "Old Soldier" looking over the burial ground with an empty left sleeve, balding head, and weary face, representing the "universal" soldier of the War of 1812. The granite pedestal on which he rests was designed by Toronto architect Frank Darling.

Walter Allward's War of 1812 "universal" soldier monument. [Caitlin McWilliams]

(D) There are several monuments and plaques within walking distance from the Fort York area. If you walk south down Bathurst St. you will come across the toy soldiers of *"Monument to the War of 1812."* (*GPS – 600 Fleet St. Toronto, ON*) In 2008, Vancouver-based artist and author Douglas Coupland revealed this four metre high sculpture of two toy soldiers, one standing and one fallen. The standing soldier is painted gold and depicts a

Tour

member of the 1813 Royal Newfoundland Regiment. The other soldier is painted silver and depicts an American soldier from the 16th U.S. Infantry Regiment. The statue pays tribute to the men who defended Fort York against American invasion.

A night capture of the toy soldiers monument in downtown Toronto. [Caitlin McWilliams]

(E) Your next stop reflects on the second invasion of York. Turn right on Fleet St. and continue walking until you reach Coronation Park at the foot of Stratchan Ave. Along the road on the east side, an Ontario Heritage Trust plaque that describes the action. (*GPS – 750 Lake Shore Blvd. West, Toronto, ON*) In July 1813, the village was attacked, for a second time, by 300 American soldiers retreating from Burlington Heights. The invaders pillaged the town and burned an encampment on Gibraltar Point (modern day Toronto Islands) before continuing their retreat.

(F) A Historic Sites and Monuments Board plaque commemorating the defence of York is located at the south end of the Liberty Grand at Exhibition Place on the stone lion pillar. (*GPS – 210 Princes' Blvd. Toronto, ON*) The plaque acknowledges the specific regiments and Aboriginals who fought in the April battle. To access this plaque, cross Strachan Ave. from Coronation Park and enter the Exhibition Place fairgrounds. Take Princes' Blvd. into the park and follow signs for "Liberty Grand Entertainment Complex."

(G) If you happen to be on the west side of the city, close to Old York, spend some time at the new 1812 interpretation centre opened in the summer of 2012 by Ontario Heritage Trust. (*GPS – 210 Front St. East, Toronto, ON*) The information centre/museum is located on the site of Ontario's first parliament buildings which were burned down during the American occupation of York. The exhibits here revolve around items found during archaeological excavations, including remnants of burnt timbers from the original structure.

Hamilton

Burlington

Lake Ontario

Queen Elizabeth Way

Hamilton & Scourge
Naval Memorial Gardens

Stoney Creek

Niagara
Escarpment

Battlefield Park
National Historic
Site

C

Stoney
Creek
Cemetery

D

E

Red Hill Valley
Parkway

Hamilton

Lincon M. Alexander
Parkway

Dundurn Castle
National Historic Site

A

B

Hamilton
Cemetery

York
Boulevard

Ancaster

Wilson Street
East

Ancaster

Ancaster Assize
Monument

F

Wilson Street
East

N

Hamilton

A day tour through the Hamilton region will take you to the battlefields of Burlington Heights, Stoney Creek, and Ancaster. You will begin beneath Burlington Heights, 30 metres above Burlington Bay. This was the front line and main staging area for British forces operating in Southwestern Upper Canada and the Niagara Peninsula from 1813 until 1815. In June 1813, close to 1,600 British troops turned the area into a fortified supply depot and defensive post. Though considered a "jumping off point" for further action, the grounds never saw battle. On 6 June 1813, 700 British troops marched from Burlington Heights and attacked the American encampment. During the 40-minute battle, hundreds of soldiers were killed and two American brigadier generals were captured. Overwhelmed and defeated, the American army retreated to Forty Mile Creek (Grimsby), a move which ended American operations on the Niagara Frontier. The Battle of Stoney Creek was a crucial British victory that prevented the Americans from seizing Upper Canada.

(A) Dundurn Castle National Historic Site is the first stop. (*GPS – Dundurn Castle National Historic Site, 610 York Blvd. Hamilton, ON*) To begin the tour from Toronto, take the 403 West to the Main St. exit. Turn left onto Dundurn until York Blvd, and turn left here to access the parking lot at the north end of the estate. Richard Beasley, one of Canada's first settlers, built a modest house on this property in 1810. In 1812, the military commandeered the grounds and the existing structures for the defence of the colony. In 1835, Sir Allan Napier MacNab used the Beasley foundation to build the 18,000 square foot Dundurn Castle you see today. The house now functions as a furnished house museum which illustrates grand country life in 1855.

Dundurn Castle. [Caitlin McWilliams]

Since the end of the War of 1812, Dundurn Castle has passed through many owners but its link to the conflict remains. The unique site has incorporated the surviving military earthworks and ruins into the landscape and even in the basement of the house. Two lines of earthworks, a 2.5 metre deep ditch with ridges rising over four metres above the ground, were designed to funnel the invaders into several killing zones open to cannon and musket fire. The killing zones are best seen in courtyard near a former gun battery. Another section is visible on the south lawn in line with the one in the courtyard, and a third rises slightly from the ground on the north lawn. Deep in the cellar the structure of the original military buildings have been preserved. A brick archway, a small ammunition magazine, and a large gun powder magazine are embedded in the foundation of the house.

The ideal visit to the site lasts at least two hours with an hour reserved for the guided tour that takes you into the Castle. Be sure to walk the grounds after your tour. Informative plaques, concentrated along its northern perimeter and inside the courtyard, help to add context to what you are seeing. Be sure to stop by the cluster of memorials just north of the parking and picnic area along the fence line, past the first canon. It includes a monument to General Vincent and a marker indicating the defensive earthwork startline. If you are unable to visit the site in person, you can take an interactive virtual tour of the grounds and buildings at museumshamilton.com.

The Hamilton Military Museum, located on-site, includes a number of artefacts from the grounds. Housed in the former MacNab gate house near the corner of York and Dundurn, the museum combines hands-on activities with traditional exhibits on the War of 1812. There are also exhibits on the Rebellion of 1837 and 1838, the Boer War, and the First World War. The museum also features an appointment-only library and archives on Canada's military past.

B If you have time, walk across York Blvd. to the Hamilton Cemetery. (*GPS – Hamilton Cemetery, 777 York Blvd. Hamilton,*

On the edge of the grounds at Dundurn Castle. [Caitlin McWilliams]

Tour

ON) During the War of 1812, local militiamen and Iroquois warriors camped here and the ramparts that protected them are still visible. Look for the headstones of Sarah Cooke, "Hamilton's Laura Secord," and James and Mary Gage, whose farm was annexed by Americans during the Battle of Stoney Creek.

(C) The Stoney Creek battleground has been preserved near Centennial Pwky. and King St. as Battlefield Park, a National Historic Site (1960) spanning 32 acres of serene greenspace. (GSP – *Battlefield Park, 77 King St. West, Stoney Creek, ON)* The site is divided into east and west parts by Battlefield Creek. The Battle of Stoney Creek is re-enacted here annually on the weekend closest to 6 June. You can also view the site online at museumshamilton.com/Hamilton-civic-museums.html.

Gage Homestead is the beautiful log and wood dwelling located at the south-east corner of the park. Approximately 3,500 American soldiers camped in the Gage family homestead which stood right in the middle of

The Battle of Stoney Creek Monument. [Caitlin McWilliams]

the battlefield. During this time the house was plundered of its housewares, livestock, and even its whiskey. The house was abandoned until 1899 when a relative of the family purchased the property and transferred it to the Women's Wentworth Historical Society who opened it as the Battlefield House Museum. In the 1970s the Niagara Parks Commission restored the house to reflect the 1835 period. Today, the house is owned by the City of Stoney Creek and functions as a "living history museum" that interprets the daily life of the Gage family and the history of the Battle of Stoney Creek. Beyond the house tree-lined paths, flowerbeds, and a tall flight of flagstone steps lead upwards to the Battle of Stoney Creek Monument, the second largest built in Canada to commemorate the War of 1812.

The Women's Wentworth Historical Society was largely responsible for the Battle of Stoney Creek Monument. The Queenston limestone structure is modeled after the Admiral Nelson Monument in Edinburgh, Scotland, and was unveiled on the 100th anniversary of the battle. The tapering octagonal tower rises above the ridge at a symbolic one hundred feet. Inside, a spiral staircase leads to the observation deck and a dramatic view of the battlefield. Around the monument are eight stone shields inscribed with a names of important figures in the War of 1812.

A second memorial, the "Lion's Monument" sits across the street on the elevated ground where the British positioned their artillery during the battle – known at the time as Smith's Knoll. Unveiled in 1910, the monument is

The "Lion's Monument" at Smith's Knoll. [Caitlin McWilliams]

Tour

a four metre-high fieldstone pyramid cairn topped with a limestone slab and a sandstone lion. A tomb-shaped memorial in honour of the American war dead at the Battle of Stoney Creek was added just left of the pyramid in 1979. In 1999, an archaeological dig uncovered bits of cloth and more than 80 uniform buttons, leading researchers to conclude that this was likely a mass grave for American and British soldiers killed at Stoney Creek. In 2000, the area was rededicated as a National Historic Site and the remains were placed in a new crypt and reinterred and the five British cannons surrounding the site were restored.

D The most modest of the monuments in this area lies in the Stoney Creek Cemetery adjacent to the park. (*GPS – Stoney Creek Cemetery, 2880 King St. East Stoney Creek, Hamilton, ON*) From Smith's Knoll travel right, cross onto the south side at Centennial, and turn left into the cemetery. On the right side, about six stones from the entrance, sits a two metre tall granite pillar. The monument, dedicated in 1938, marks the site of initial contact and memorialize three men who contributed to victory at Stoney Creek: Billy "The Scout" Green, Isaac Corman, and General Harvey.

E Stop next at the Hamilton & Scourge Navy Memorial Garden in Centennial Park. From Battlefield Park travel north on Centennial Pwky. past the QEW and turn left onto Van Wagners Beach Rd., then right onto Confederation Dr. (*GPS – 680 Confederation Dr. Hamilton ON*) Make sure to turn right at the fork and park in the lot adjacent to the memorial.

In honour of Billy Green, Isaac Corman, and General Harvey. [Caitlin McWilliams]

The Navy Memorial Garden commemorates the loss of 53 American sailors who died on the morning of 8 August 1813 when two United States merchant schooners, the USS *Hamilton* and the USS *Scourge*, capsized during a sudden storm. It was the largest loss of life suffered by the U.S. Navy in a single engagement during the War of 1812 on Lake Ontario. The wrecks were discovered in 1975 approximately 11km northwest of the Port Dalhousie near St. Catharines. The remnants were found virtually intact and preserved in 300 feet of freezing water. Though not considered a formal gravesite, it is likely that the wrecks still house the human remains. Today the vessels remain at the bottom of Lake Ontario as a National Historic Site, and the City of Hamilton is deliberating on a comprehensive plan for research, conservation, and education of the site.

At this serene site, established in 1938, 53 white headstones, much like those found in other war cemeteries, flank a nautical flagpole reminiscent of the foremast of the *Scourge*. Each grave is marked with a circular bronze commemoration plaque placed by the National Society United States Daughters of 1812, an American women's service organization. A descriptive Historic Sites plaque stands to the left of the site, and a small bronze plaque lies to the right for Archie Hodge, the captain of the research team that discovered the wrecks. A third plaque is scheduled to be unveiled in 2013 in conjunction with an exhibit at the Hamilton Art Museum showcasing naval paintings, scale models, and sonar photos of the wrecks.

The graveyard at the Navy Memorial Garden. [Caitlin McWilliams]

(F) The enthusiast will want to make one final stop in Ancaster. On the tip of a small park sits a monument to the Ancaster Assize. (*GPS – 360 Wilson St. East, Ancaster, ON*) The story of the Ancaster Eight, regardless of if you visit, is worth contemplating and highlights the questions of loyalty during the War of 1812. In 1813, the British Militia captured a number of marauders in a house near Chatham Ontario. At least 15 of the men were residents of Upper Canada before the war. Their actions in a time of war threatened the stability of the young colony. On these grounds in 1814, 19 men were convicted of high treason – 11 were exiled to the United States and the other eight sentenced to be hung. At the hanging the presiding judge announced "You are to be drawn on Hurdles to place of execution, hanged by the neck but not until dead, cut down while alive and your entrails taken out and burnt before your faces, your heads cut off bodies divided into four quarters, heads and quarters to be at the King's disposal." The trial marked by a lonely plaque in Ancaster, is representative of the conflicting views on the war in the colony. Those differing views have been minimized and virtually ignored in the history and memory that remains of the War of 1812.

The Bloody Assize. [Johanna Boeringa]

Niagara-on-the-Lake

New York

St. Mark's Anglican Church and Cemetery

Fort George National Historic Site Ⓐ

Queens

Ⓑ

Front Street

Wellington Street

Fort Mississauga National Historic Site Ⓒ

Picton Street

Ⓔ

Niagara Historical Society and Museum

Niagara-on-the-Lake ●

Mississauga Street

Mary Street

King Street

Lakeshore Road

Butler's Burial Site

Ⓓ

Buttler Street

N

Ontario

Image © 2013 TerraMetrics

Niagara-on-the-Lake

(A) Begin at Fort George National Historic Site on the edge of Niagara-on-the-Lake. (*GPS – 26 Queen's Parade, Niagara-on-the-Lake, ON*) Reconstruction of the site has been ongoing since the 1930s and today the fort appears how it did from 1796-1799. The site consists of seven buildings surrounded by palisades, earthworks, and canons. With Fort Niagara visible from the ramparts, the site offers an opportunity to appreciate the importance of fortified positions in the war.

Tours take place every hour and introduce visitors to garrison life in the early 19th century. The musket firing is not to be missed as the costumed guide takes you through the challenges of using a smooth bore weapon. The staff are dressed in the uniforms of the 41st Regiment of Foot. Note that there is a cairn and plaque describing the battle about three kilometres northwest of Fort George, near the shore of Lake Ontario on the northwest end of Queen St. The fort is open on weekends from April to October and admission is free. See the Parks Canada website for more detailed information.

(B) From Fort George, travel down Prideaux St. past Wellington St. to historic St. Mark's Anglican Church and Cemetery. (*GPS – 41 Byron, Niagara-on-the-Lake, ON*) The church was used as a hospital and storehouse during the American occupation of the town and the trenches that are visible throughout the churchyard were dug for American defences. Upon their retreat, the American forces burned the church along with the rest of the town, but only the roof succumbed.

The weathered grave of William Dickson at St. Mark's Anglican Church. [Caitlin McWilliams]

A careful walk through the elm and willow trees will reveal the badly weathered headstones of men who fell at Queenston Heights and in nearby battles. In the porch near the north door of the church is a fallen tablet that memorializes three British soldiers who died on 27 May 1813 at the Battle of Fort George. Nearby is the stone of John McFarland, who was taken prisoner at the capture of Fort George and whose property was destroyed in the burning of Niagara. Also look for the burial of Captain Copeland Radcliffe of His Britannic Majesty's Navy, who was killed attempting to overtake an American vessel at the Battle of Baltimore 12 August 1814. The flat headstones of Charles Morrison and Geo Forsythe are alleged to have been used by American cooks as chopping blocks and if you look close you will see that the stones do have some peculiar scars. In 2005, a marker was placed at the gravesite of the Honourable William Dickson. The future member of Upper Canada's Legislative was taken prisoner when American forces invaded Newark and sent to Albany in the United States.

Walk along the south entrance path and look for "Brock's Seat," a large stone with granite marker. Legend has it that early in the War of 1812, Brock sat on this stone by the edge of the Niagara River as he contemplated American intentions. In November 1893, William Kirby, a poet, had the rock moved to St. Mark's Cemetery. A formal marker recognizing the stone's significance was placed next to it in June 2011. Under a tree at the north entrance lies a 2012 granite marker to commemorate all members of the Militia and the British Army who fought in the War of 1812 and lie in marked and unmarked graves near the site.

(C) Continue down Prideaux St. a short distance to Fort Mississauga National Historic Site. The site is well worth the walk down the winding trail through the Niagara-on-the-Lake Golf Club on Mississauga Point. (*GPS – 223 Queen St. Niagara-on-the-Lake, ON*) The first lighthouse on the Great Lakes was built near here in 1804, but was torn down to make room for Fort Mississauga after retreating American forces destroyed the town and Fort George in December 1813. The tower is the only structure remaining today and was constructed of bricks salvaged from both the lighthouse and the rubble of the town. Fort Mississauga is the only example in Canada of a square tower within a star shaped earthwork, and today the site offers visitors a look at a fortification from the era that has undergone very little restoration since it was built. A moat still encircles the ramparts that are believed to have protected seven structures including five barracks, a cook house, and the stone tower. Two powder magazines are built into the earthworks on either side of the gate, and a sallyport extends under the earthworks on the side facing Lake Ontario. The site is maintained by Parks Canada and is accessible via a pedestrian trail that starts at the corner of Simcoe and Front Streets. There are a few exterior display panels that help interpret the site. Fort Niagara in Youngstown is clearly visible from the ramparts and the view allows for an understanding the strategic importance of the site.

The remains of Fort Mississauga. [Caitlin McWilliams]

D From here, cross Queen St. and follow Butler St. which ends at Butler's Burial Site, located in Two Mile Creek Conservation Area. (*GPS – 538 Butler St. Niagara-on-the-Lake, ON*) The site is named after Lieutenant Colonel John Butler, founder of Niagara-on-the-Lake and organizer of the Loyalist Corps known as Butler's Rangers. Here in 1813, 23 soldiers from the U.S. 13th Infantry, along with their commander Lieutenant Samuel Elridge, were killed on these grounds by a band of Six Nations and Western Indians. Today there is a plaque commemorating Butler and a monument to the soldiers killed in 1813. A number of Butler's family members are buried here, behind the monument.

E The Niagara Historical Society and Museum makes for a convenient final stop if you intend to travel out of Niagara-on-the-Lake via the Niagara Pwky. (*GPS – 43 Castlereagh St. Niagara-on-the-Lake, ON*) The museum revolves around the history of the Niagara-on-the-Lake community and houses an extensive collection of items and documents relating to the area's involvement in the War of 1812. Their most recognized artefact is Brock's felt and ostrich feather hat. It arrived after his death so it was never worn by him, but it was placed on his coffin during his funerals in 1824 and 1853. The museum is open year-round and researchers are encouraged to make an appointment to view their archival resources.

Queenston Heights

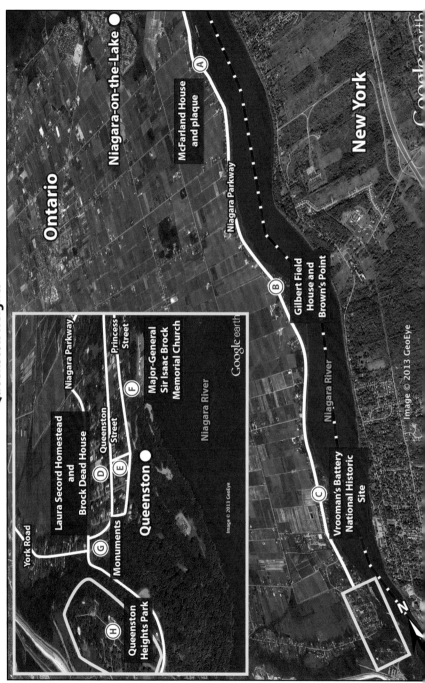

Queenston Heights

(A) While travelling south towards Queenston Heights via the Niagara Pwky., you may wish to stop briefly to view the McFarland House and plaque describing the capture of Fort Niagara. (*GPS – 15927 Niagara Pwky. Niagara-on-the-Lake, ON*) The red brick residence was built in 1800 by James McFarland, whose grave is the one seen previously at St. Mark's Cemetery. During the War of 1812, his home was converted into a hospital and used by both British and American forces. The house was restored by the Niagara Parks Commission and portrays life in Niagara between 1800 and 1830. Guided tours of the home are available from mid May until September. A British battery was also located on the property, and a ravine was the launch point for the British attack on Fort Niagara in 1813. A plaque describing this victory is just a few minutes walk north, along the gorge across the road from Kurtz Orchards County Market.

(B) About 3.5km further down the Niagara Pwky. you may choose to stop to view two markers indicating the locations of the Gilbert Field House and Brown's Point. (*GPS – 15287 Niagara Pwky. Niagara-on-the-Lake, ON*) The Field House was used as a barracks and hospital by British forces and was subjected to a brief bombardment from an American battery. Though damaged, it was one of few houses in the area to survive the hostilities and has survived on the hill just behind the plaque. A short distance south, along the Niagara Pwky. Recreational Trail, is a 1915 stone which marks the place where Brock allegedly called out, on his way to Queenston Heights 13 October 1812, "Push on, brave York Volunteers."

(C) Vrooman's Battery, a National Historic Site since 1921, is also along the way to Queenston Heights. (*GPS – 14759 Niagara River Pwky. Queenston, ON*) When the American army attempted to cross the Niagara River, they were warded off by British Army regulars and Canadian militia. Two artillery positions provided support for the infantry and Vrooman's Battery, firing from Vrooman's Point, was one of them. Today the site consists of a stone marker and National Monuments and Historic Sites plaque along the roadway, and a slight mound on the bank of the river. It is worthwhile to stop at this elevated position to help in understanding the strategic position of the battery.

(D) Begin your journey through the village of Queenston at the Laura Secord Homestead. (*GPS – 29 Queenston St. Niagara-on-the-Lake, ON*). During the Battle of Queenston Heights, the house was ransacked by invading American soldiers. In June the following year, Laura left her house to begin her now famous 32km trek to warn the British of the impending American surprise attack. The house was reconstructed in 1971 by Laura Secord Inc. to match the original structure.

A visit to the homestead offers an opportunity to engage with middle-class life during the early 19th century. Take special note of items like the numberless cards in the common area and the moralistic cards with verses from the Bible in the fancier living room. Artefacts like the iron, the open fire kitchen, the small bedroom and bathing station, and the small blue wrapped cone of expensive white sugar (a sign of prestige in 1812) help understand the life in 1812. The guides, always dressed in early 19th century attire, are fantastic. The constant reference to the origin of many of our commonly used expressions – like "settle down," a term used for your guests, usually of a lower class than yourself, that slept on the straw bed in the common area – make the experience memorable. A stone marker sits on the east side of the Secord property and was placed by the Women's Literary Club of St. Catharines in 1901. There is also a plaque at south end. The house is open from May to October, and note that only the main floor of the house is wheelchair accessible.

A look at the moralistic playing cards at the Laura Secord Homestead. [Matt Symes]

(E) At the intersection of Queenston St. and Partition St. is the "Brock Dead House." (*GPS – 20 Queenston St. Niagara-on-the-Lake, ON*) Brock's body was taken immediately after his death. Though the original house was town down in the 1920s, archival documents and surviving photographs link Brock to the site. In 2011, a formal recognition was held by the Queenston Residents Association who placed a large square stone mounted plaque on the corner of the existing property. The house is a private property today, but a stop here will help you visualize the chaos and formalities that occurred following Brock's death.

F Travel east on Partition Rd. and left on Princess St. until you reach St. Savior Anglican Church, or the Major-General Sir Isaac Brock Memorial Church. (*GPS – 12 Princess St. Niagara-on-the-Lake, ON*) The parish has existed since 1817, but the first church was destroyed by lightening in 1839. The first Bishop of Niagara, Thomas Brock Fuller, godson of Major-General Sir Isaac Brock, consecrated this building in 1879. The charming stone building has the same name of the church in Brock's birthplace of Guernsey, Channel Islands, and a twinning ceremony was held in 2012 to formally recognize the connection with a monument. Another stone and plaque site next to this one and describes the history of the church and was placed in 1977. The Queenston Residents Association placed a new plaque on the lawn in 2012 describing Brock as the "Hero of Canada." Just a few minutes down the road is a trail leading to the Queenston boat launch docks on the Niagara River. At the water level here you can easily gain some perspective of the elevated cliff of Queenston Heights and see the close proximity of the United States-Canada border.

Major-General Sir Isaac Brock Memorial Church. [Caitlin McWilliams]

G As you continue toward Queenston Heights, stop at the very edge of the village in the shadow of the cliff stands two monuments – one for Brock and one for his horse Alfred. (*GPS – 1 Queenston St. Niagara-on-the-Lake, ON*) This stone cenotaph indicates the spot where Brock fell during his second attempt to recapture Queenston Heights. It was dedicated by the Prince of Wales (future King Edward VII) His Royal Highness Albert Edward on 18 September 1860. Brock's massive monument looms in the distance and there are steps leading to a trail that winds up the cliff face. Beside Brock's

Tour

marker is a 1976 monument to his horse, which features a miniature bronze horse statue encased in glass atop a sandstone pillar.

A 1914 photo of the stone cenotaph that marks where Brock fell. [F. Petire Collection, Niagara Falls Public Library, 102192]

(H) Stop next at Queenston Heights Park. (*GPS – 14184 Queenston St. Niagara-on-the-Lake, ON*) If you choose the long winding trail, five interpretive plaques highlight several key stages of the battle. Following this trail offers the chance to understand the folly of Brock's charge and the value of Sheaffe's encircling move to reach the high ground. You will see the Redan Battery monument along the way, composed of three stones and a plaque that marks the approximate location of John Macdonell's death. The park features numerous plaques and monuments recognizing significant figures of the battle. The Brock Monument, where the General and Macdonell are buried, is the obvious centrepiece. A 40 metre monument once stood on the site but was destroyed in 1840 by an explosive charge. The 56 metre cut stone granite memorial that stands today was completed in 1856. It is now staffed by the Friends of Fort George and guides offer a highly coloured version of the events that occurred here. A climb to the top of the fluted column and its 235 spiral steps is recommended for those with young legs. The same beautiful view down the river can be seen from a great viewing area just outside the park. Inside the monument are a number of brass plaques and the two bodies are interred in crypts within the walls. Atop the monument is a 4.9 metre statue of Brock in a heroic pose facing the United States. You can climb to the top of the monument between May and September.

Various Historic Sites and Monuments Board plaques surround Brock's Monument. Near the Queenston Heights Restaurant is a monument commemorating Laura Secord. The four-sided column overlooks the Niagara River and the village of Queenston. This was the second monument built in her honour in Niagara, the first which is located at her gravesite in Drummond Hill Cemetery near Lundy's Lane. Look also for the plaque commemorating the site of Fort Drummond near the west corner. There is also a plaque describing the Brock monument along the walking path near the roundabout.

A 1969 aerial photo of the Brock memorial. [Niagara Falls Public Library, 363685]

Tour

Niagara

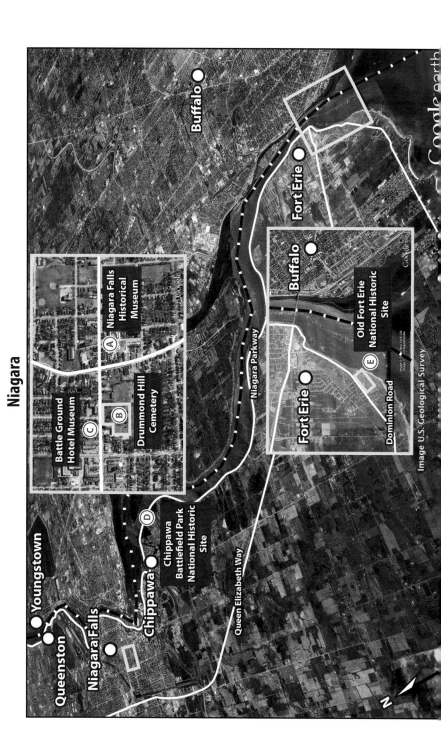

Youngstown

Queenston

Niagara Falls

Chippawa

Buffalo

Fort Erie

Niagara Parkway

Queen Elizabeth Way

A - Niagara Falls Historical Museum

B - Drummond Hill Cemetery

C - Battle Ground Hotel Museum

D - Chippawa Battlefield Park National Historic Site

Buffalo

Fort Erie

E - Old Fort Erie National Historic Site

Dominion Road

Image U.S. Geological Survey

N

208

(A) From Queenston follow the Niagara Pwky. to Niagara Falls and Lundy's Lane. Stop first at the Niagara Falls Historical Museum. (*GPS – 5810 Ferry St. Niagara Falls, ON*) The museum reopened in a brand new and modern glass facility in the summer of 2012 and is only closed on Monday. The new 1812 gallery offers an overview of the battles in the area through displays that celebrate Niagara's local history. Anyone interested in how the memory of Lundy's Lane has evolved over time will certainly find the exhibit space interesting. There are a wide-range of unique artefacts on displays including the original oil painting portrait of Brock and a piece of Brock's first coffin. Upstairs, the exhibits on power generation and Niagara Falls as a honeymoon capital are good fun and rife with popular ephemera. The museum also has a small movie theatre that plays rotating Niagara-related films daily. The parking lot behind the museum is an ideal spot to leave your vehicle and begin a walking tour of the Lundy's Lane battlefield.

(B) Drummond Hill Cemetery sits on the elevated ground where the British main position was located and contains a few major monuments. (*GPS – 6110 Lundy's Lane. Niagara Falls, ON*) Walk west down Lundy's Lane towards the Drummond Rd. and Portage Rd. intersection and enter at the gates off of the sidewalk. The cemetery existed before the Battle of Lundy's Lane but became known as Drummond Hill in honour of General Drummond who led the charge. His grave is easy to spot because of the miniature horse sculpture. The cemetery is also the final resting place of Laura Secord. Her striking 2.4 metre high monument features a detailed bronze bust and cannot be missed. Among multiple British and American

A 1938 photo of the Drummond Hill Cemetery. [Niagara Falls Public Library, 91117]

Laura Secord's grave in Drummond Hill Cemetery. [Caitlin McWilliams]

War of 1812 graves sits an elegant 1895 monument to the men who fought and in honour of the 22 British soldiers who are buried in a vault beneath it. In 1938, three bronze plaques were posted to the monument and bear the names of those who were killed at Lundy's Lane. In the summer of 2004, four limestone panels were posted on the cemetery wall that faces Lundy's Lane. The slabs depict scenes from the battle and marked the 190th anniversary.

C On the Lundy's Lane battleground sits the Battle Ground Hotel Museum, located directly across from Drummond Hill. (*GPS – 6151 Lundy's Lane. Niagara Falls, ON*) The tavern-hotel functioned as an early form of commemoration by serving veterans and visitors to the battlefield in the immediate post-war era. Today the restored structure is the only surviving 19th century tavern-hotel in Ontario. Artefacts from the area illustrate life during the War of 1812 and are used to explore early Niagara tourism. Tours of the museum are offered from May to October.

D From Lundy's Lane, travel towards Fort Erie via the Niagara Pwky. On your way you may wish to stop at Chippawa Battlefield Park and National Historic Site in Chippawa Village. (*GPS – 8709 Niagara Pwky. Niagara Falls, ON*) When you cross the bridge take a look at the river which in 1814 provided a significant natural barrier to an American advance to Fort George. Major-General Phineas Riall's decision to abandon this position, cross the river, and confront the Americans in an open field defies easy explanation.

In 1995, the Niagara Parks Commission acquired the 121 hectares of land where the battle was fought and created a self-guided walking tour through the park and wooded area. Display panels help interpret the site and allow you to appreciate the ranges at which such battles were fought. The limestone cairn is the focus of the battlefield. It is dedicated to the regiments and First

Tour

Nations warriors who fought in the battle and commemorating the peace that has prevailed between Canada and the United States since that time. A tall Historic Sites and Monument Board plaque is situated along the east side of the park near the Niagara River Recreation Trail. The picturesque park is open year-round and a memorial service is held on 5 July each year.

(E) Continue south to Fort Erie which began as a British outpost in 1764. The first stone fortifications were built in 1804. (*GPS – 350 Lakeshore Rd. Fort Erie, ON*) Transformed into a heap of ruins when the British retreated from the Niagara in 1813, it was partially rebuilt after the British victories at Stoney Creek and Fort Niagara. When the Americans under General Jacob Brown returned in July 1814, Fort Erie surrendered. American engineers created more extensive fortifications which helped the garrison to withstand the British siege of August 1814. Old Fort Erie, owned by the Niagara Parks commission, offers some of the very best guided tours using history students who are knowledgeable as well as enthusiastic. The tour begins with a video drawn from the excellent PBS documentary on the War of 1812.

Entrance to the old park and battle memorial to the "Heroes who fell during the Fort Erie Siege." [F. Petire Collection, Niagara Falls Public Library, 96288]

Youngstown, NY & Erie, PA

Ontario

Lake Ontario

Robert Moses Parkway

Fort Niagara

A

B 1812 Cemetery

Niagara River

Google earth

Queenston

Niagara Falls

Niagara River

Buffalo

Fort Erie

Lake Erie

New York

Google earth

Presque Isle State Park

Erie Maritime Museum

C

Bayfront Parkway

West 8th Street

79

Erie

Peninsula Drive

Erie

© 2013 Cnes/Spot Image
Image NOAA

N

Crossing the Border: Youngstown, NY & Erie, PA

(A) Fort Niagara's history dates back to the early French settlers who built a stockade at this strategic point in 1687. (*GPS – 4 Scott Ave. Youngstown, NY*) The fort was abandoned the following year after a harsh winter, but in 1726 the large stone structure that still dominated the grounds was constructed. It was named the "House of Peace" and made to look like a trading post to appease the Iroquois. In reality, it was a heavily defended fortress designed to deter a First Nations attack. Today it is the most imposing building in Fort Niagara and you can easily imagine the generations of French, British, and American officers that stayed there. Little reconstruction has been done, and the fireplaces are still blackened from centuries of use.

From Fort Niagara you can see across the river to Fort George in Niagara-on-the-Lake in Ontario. On a clear day, you might be able to peer north across Lake Ontario's waters and see the Toronto skyline, giving you an idea how close York, and all of Southeastern Ontario, was to the American border in 1812. The fort was surrendered to the Americans in 1796 after the signing of the Jay Treaty, the same Treaty that relinquished control of Fort Mackinac far to the east. It was captured by the British on 19 December 1813, and held until the Treaty of Ghent.

A view of Fort Niagara from the Canadian side. [Matt Symes]

(B) The "1812 Cemetery," or the Military Cemetery at Old Fort Niagara, contains the graves of soldiers, and some civilians, who where stationed there as early as the 18th century. Walk east from the fort along Scott Ave. until just before the Officer's Club. Note that the road is a dead end. Many of the known graves date from the War of 1812 period, including "John Crystie" and "Adgt. Thos. Poe, Penn. Vols." A large stone crypt-shaped monument commemorates the unknown American soldiers and sailors killed in the area during the War of 1812. The cemetery is maintained by the Old Fort Niagara Association and open daily. See oldfortniagara.org for more information.

Crossing the border at Buffalo, there are two roads you can take to Erie, Pennsylvania. The first is the major highway, the I-90 which will save you about 30 minutes of driving time. The second, and the one we suggest on the tour, is the Seaway Route which wanders along the coast of Lake Erie and is far more scenic. After you are finished touring the museum, you may wish to round the peninsula and visit Presque Ile State Park. Looping across the water in front of the city's harbour, the peninsula was where Commodore Perry built six ships of the nine that eventually wrestled control of the lake from the Royal Navy. You can visit the Perry Monument and visit the beach there if the weather is nice.

Erie was where the American navy constructed the fleet that would wrest control of the Lake from the British. The Battle of Lake Erie on 10 September 1813, was the first time a British squadron had been captured in its entirety by an enemy force and cemented American domination on the Great Lakes. The American commodore, Oliver Hazard Perry, became an instant hero of the war for his victory over the British.

(C) Touring a naval battlefield is not easy, but in the case of the Battle of Lake Erie the bicentennial "celebration" planned for August-September 2013 offers the opportunity to enlist as a crew member for an elaborate re-enactment. Visit battleoflakeerie-bicentennial.com provides information about the events.

Two sites associated with the battle are worth visiting at any time. Put-in-Bay, on the Island of South Bass, Ohio, was the temporary naval base used by Commodore Perry before the battle. The National Park Services manages the "Perry Victory and International Peace Memorial" a 107 metre high tower with an observation platform providing striking views of the island and Lake Erie. A visitor centre offers balanced information about Oliver Hazzard Perry and the battle. Put-in-Bay is a major tourist destination in the summer months so reservations are a must. See visitputinbay.com for more information and the necessary links to ferry service and accommodation.

The lake's history during the War of 1812 is explained at the Erie Maritime Museum where the US Brig *Niagara* is docked. *(GPS – 150 E Front St. #100, Erie, PA)* For $8.00 you can enter the museum, and if it's not out on the water, you will also be able to tour the US Brig *Niagara*. The museum, located within a former power plant, offers a number of informative exhibits on the War of 1812 as well as the first iron-hulled ship of the U.S. Navy, the USS *Michigan*. Not surprisingly, it focuses on the local naval history of the lake. for more information visiteriemaritimemuseum.org.

If you have time Presque Isle State Park, which encompasses the sandy Penninsula that served to protect the construction of Perry's fleet, is one of the great nature centres on Lake Erie and one of the top five birding spots in the United States. The Tom Ridge Environmental Centre offers an introduction to the park. Visit presqueilse.org for more information.

The US Brig *Niagara* at the Erie Maritime Museum. [Nick Lachance]

Touring Québec

Tour

216

Touring Québec

Compared to Ontario, the War of 1812 is not well remembered in Québec. Whereas Upper Canadian Loyalists remembered the war as proof of their loyalty to Britain, the Canadiens of Lower Canada were not so eager to glorify the conflict. It remained a British war fought for British objectives, not anything particular to the French Canadians themselves. Even in light of the success of Charles de Salaberry, the War of 1812 had virtually no influence on the already established French Canadian identity. The centennial celebrations had no room for French Canada and the overt nationalism of the 1920s and 1930s memorialization found no voice in a deeply resentful Québec.

Instead, the war was grouped with other British conflicts and became more a symbol of continued British rule over French Canadians than a symbol of their loyalty. While some certainly celebrated their military role, it was largely ignored by the majority of French Canadians through the 19th and 20th centuries. The political agenda during the 200th anniversary has attempted to craft a shared understanding of the war but the rejection of official commemorative efforts in Québec remains the same. The result is far less commemoration of the war in the province, despite being a key theatre during the War of 1812.

The tour of Québec is certainly worth the trip and the Québécois culture is wonderful to experience. The entire tour consists of a lot of driving but the scenery of these important sites along the St. Lawrence makes for a picturesque and quintessential Canadian road trip.

The St. Lawrence River along L'Isle-aux-Coudres. [Jean Hemond]

Coteau-du-Lac

Châteauguay, Lacolle & L'Île-aux-Noix

(A) Begin your trip to the battlefields of Lower Canada at Coteau-du-Lac National Historic Site. (*GPS – 308 A Chemin du Fleuve. Coteau-du-Lac, QC*) Coteau-du-Lac is a small city on the north shore of the St. Lawrence River and is the location of the first canal lock system in North America. Although Coteau-du-Lac did not see any action during the War of 1812, it played a major role in defending the river and the border region. In 1813, existing structures were expanded and reinforced while a new blockhouse and barracks were built. A line of earthworks surrounded the fort and a pivoting platform battery of 24 artillery pieces was placed on the hill. Coteau-du-Lac became a fully functioning, clover-leaf shaped garrison manned by over 600 soldiers, whose fortified defence system was designed to protect the canal from all angles.

At the interpretation centre, a guide will use a scale model of the grounds to give a brief historical overview. Take some time to browse the small artefact exhibits on display and climb the lookout to get a good view of the site and the St. Lawrence River. None of the original fortifications of the Coteau-du-Lac bastion have been preserved, however fragments of the original foundations and earthworks are still visible. The footpath is designed to lead you through what has survived and information panels help point out what used to be the barracks, warehouse, powder magazine, and more. The earthen walls of the fort are still prominent. The replica blockhouse is one of the most popular stops and features the wartime command post during the War of 1812. The unique shape of the blockhouse allowed for clear observation of

A high dynamic range image of the blockhouse at Coteau-du-Lac. [Joanne Lévesque]

Châteauguay National Historic Site

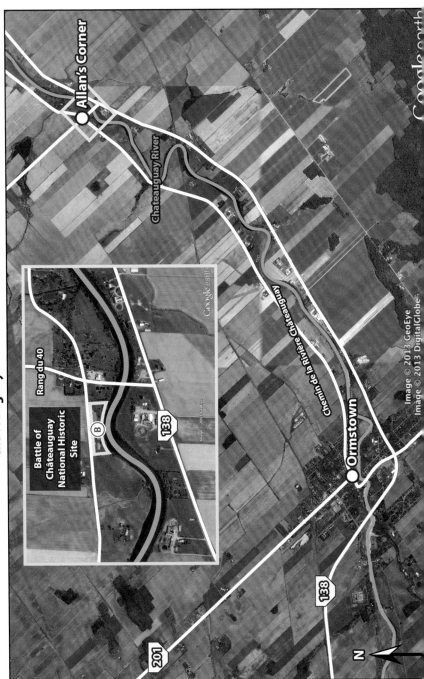

Battle of Châteauguay National Historic Site

both the water and the site itself. Inside the blockhouse there is a multimedia presentation, various exhibits and another lookout. The historic site is open from June to September.

(B) From Coteau-du-Lac, follow Autoroute 20 to Highway 201 toward Salaberry-de-Valleyfield. Stay on Highway 201 to Ormstown on the Châteauguay River. Note that there are no signs pointing to the road along the west bank of the river. Instead of following Highway 201 across the river, continue straight on Chemin Larocque and turn left on Chemin de la Rivière Châteauguay. The road along the banks of the Châteauguay River is sometimes called Rue Lampton. Pass the "Hotel de Ville" and the fairgrounds (where the Americans camped the night before the battle) to the battlefield. In 1813, the Americans advanced along this side of the river and this path will allow you to trace their route. If you wish to use the better marked tourist route, the Battle of the Châteauguay National Historic Site is well-signed on Rte. 138 as you approach Allan's Corners. The surrounding landscape has remained relatively undisturbed and the portion of the battlefield that lies outside of the Parks Canada site is mostly farmland.

The Parks Canada interpretation centre at the Châteauguay National Historic Site is located near the centre of the 500 acre battlefield. (*GPS – Châteauguay National Historic Site, 2371 Rivière-Châteauguay-Nord. Allan's Corners, QC*) A small plaque marked the site until 1973 when the Canadian government funded an initiative to build the current interpretation centre building. This building includes a museum that describes the life of a soldier during the war. The Centre also houses a viewing area of the battlefield called "The Belvedere" that includes an interactive diorama to explain the

The monument that sits on the Châteauguay River. [Linda Risacher Copp]

Tour

Lacolle Mills

events. Little attempt is made to provide context but the guide will explain the basic pattern of the action. From here you can see the monument erected by the federal government, located within walking distance of the Centre in the small community of Allan's Corners. The 39-foot high obelisk sits on the edge of the small creek that de Salaberry's men filled with abatis, tree root, and branches. This served as the equivalent of barbed wire. Parts of the creek bed are visible and it is easy to see why the position was chosen. In 1895, a granddaughter of de Salaberry unveiled the monument to a large group including family members. The Historic Sites and Monuments Board of Canada designated this location as a national historic site in 1920. For detailed information see pc.gc.ca/lhn-nhs/qc/coteaudulac/index.aspx

(C) From Allan's Corners cross the river, connect with Highway 138 toward Ormstown. Turn left on the 201 and then another left on Rte. 202. Rte. 202 is a beautiful winding two-lane road that runs along a ridge a few kilometres north of the U.S. border. This is apple orchard country with fruit and local cider for sale. Follow the signs to Lacolle on route 202 (follow the signs carefully) and then turn left on Rue de L'Église. Cross the river into Lacolle and visit the new interpretation centre focused on 1812-1814 next to the Notre-Dame-du-Mont-Carmel church. (*GPS – 27 'A' de l'Église North. Lacolle, QC*) The building is small and its exhibits limited, but from here you can understand why it was a significant defensive post. The interpretation centre is open between June and October.

(D) Next make your way to the Blockhaus de la Rivière Lacolle. (*GPS – 1, rue Principale. Saint-Paul-de-l'Île-aux-Noix, QC*) The most direct route is to head south from the interpretation centre taking a left onto Rue Van Vliet heading east. Stick right onto 1ere Ave. as the road forks and within moments you will see the blockhouse. The site was built around 1781 and became incorporated into the British defensive works during the War of

The blockhouse at Lacolle Mills. [Pierre Bona]

Fort Lennox

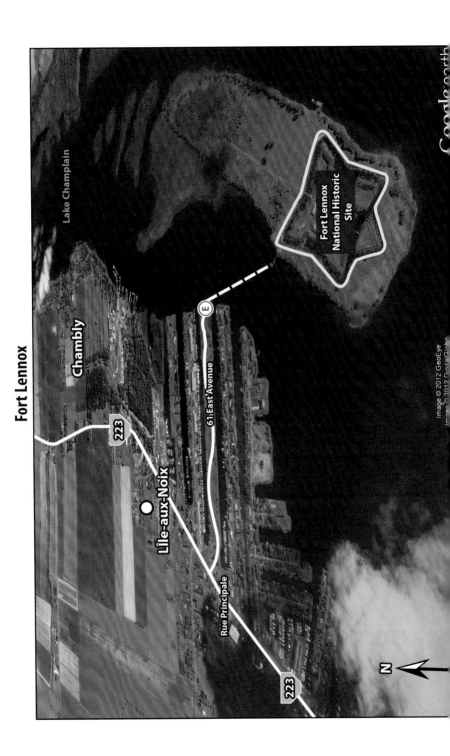

Lake Champlain

Chambly

Fort Lennox National Historic Site

223

L'Île-aux-Noix

61 East Avenue

Rue Principale

223

N

Image © 2012 GeoEye

1812. The *Blockhaus de la Rivière Lacolle* featured in several failed attempts to invade Canada. The blockhouse was designated a national historic site in 1923 and has since been renovated numerous times, most recently in 1975. Today the site is maintained by the Municipalité de St. Paul-Île-aux-Noix and staffed by young bilingual guides who know the story of both battles fought here. You can enter the blockhouse and take the guided tour from May to September.

The outpost was the scene of two battles launched to capture blockhouse as American forces advanced into Lower Canada. The shortest of the two occurred on 20 November 1812 when a small garrison of British and Canadian volunteers, aided by a band of Mohawk warriors, defended the blockhouse from an American force led by Major General Henry Dearborn. The blockhouse had been captured by Dearborn and his men in the early morning; however, a second group of American militia attempted to capture the post in the evening. During the skirmish between the two confused American groups, Charles de Salaberry and his forces launched a counterattack which forced a complete American retreat. The Americans did not attempt to retake Lacolle Mills again until 1814.

On the morning of 27 March 1814, as part of American General Wilkinson's advance into Lower Canada, Major Forsyth of the Forsyth Rifles led an advance towards the Lacolle River to capture the blockhouse and the 80 British men of the 13th Regiment of Foot who were occupying the outpost and a nearby stone mill. He reached the river on 30 March, but only after losing his 18-pounder canon in knee-high mud along the way. Outnumbered, under-equipped, and under fire, the American forces retreated by evening after enduring a lengthy barrage of British fire aided by a band of reinforcements.

E Your next stop is Fort Lennox National Historical Site on Île-aux-Noix, an important defensive base and naval shipyard island during the War of 1812. (*GPS – 1, 61e Ave. Saint-Paul-de-l'Île-aux-Noix, QC*) The fortifications served to protect the colony against American ships coming from the Richelieu River. Several warships, including the Brig *Confiance*, were constructed in the Île-aux-Noix shipyards. The Island was never actually attacked during the war, however sailors and marines stationed here captured the American ships *Growler* and *Eagle* in 1813, and Murray's Raid on Lake Champlain also began here.

The Island has been repeatedly fortified since 1759 and was occupied by a functioning garrison until 1870. A fort was built on the same site by the French during the Seven Years' War in the 1760s and these structures were modified and reinforced for use during the War of 1812 to protect the Royal Navy base at Saint-Jean. The present Fort Lennox, the third set of fortifications on the island, was built between 1819 and 1829. Throughout the 19th and 20th centuries it served multiple purposes, such as a jailhouse during the

An 1886 painting of Fort Lennox. [Henry Burnett]

1837-1838 Rebellion and a camp for German Jewish refugees during the Second World War. Fort Lennox was designated a national historic site in 1920 by the Historic Sites and Monuments Board who placed a plaque at the entrance of the grounds. In 1940, the entire island was declared a national historic park; however, the Canadian government did not begin preservation and restoration activities on the site until the 1970s.

There is no bridge to the island so you must take a short ferry ride which is included in your admission to the fort. The parking area for the ferry is well marked on Highway 223 and the boat to the island leaves every half hour. The five minute trip takes you out onto the Richilieu River and a short walk through the star-shaped moat brings you inside an elaborate 19th century fortification, part of the heavily defended border during the War of 1812. The fort is beautiful and impressively well-maintained. The guides are excellent and there are regular tours but the focus is on garrison life in the 19th century and the re-construction of the fort built between 1819 and 1829. Your guided tour will take you through the fort where you will see an 1820s period layout of the barracks, the powder magazine, the guardroom, and the prison. The north magazine features an exhibit about military engineering and restoration work carried out at the fort. The fort is open from May to October, and the guided tours are offered in both English and French.

There are many other tourist activities in the region including boat trips on the river. *Croisières Richilieu* (croisierestjean.ca) offers a river cruise that includes a stop at Fort Lennox. Children under 15 are free. At Venise-en-Québec a cruise takes you out onto the Canadian part of Lake Champlain (croisiere-lacchamplain.com). For further information about attractions, accommodations and restaurants, see regiondesaint-jean-sur-richilieu.com.

The entrance at Fort Lennox. [Linda Risacher Copp]

(F) If you wish to continue north it is worth stopping in Chambly, a picturesque city with landmarks that celebrate the life of Charles de Salaberry. De Salaberry's waterfront house has survived and can be viewed from the road. (*GPS – 18 Richelieu St. Chambly, QC*) The three storey home was built by de Salaberry between 1814 and 1815, and he lived here with his wife until his death in 1829. The 2,782 square metre lot was designated a National Historic Site in 1968 and has been completely restored for use as a private residence.

Chambly

(G) Fort Chambly National Historic Site on the Richelieu River at Chambly, Québec, and its related landmarks. (*GPS - 2 Richelieu St. Chambly, QC*) Take Highway 223 North to Saint-Jean-sur-Richelieu and then the 104 to Chambly. The square shaped stone structure is the fourth version of the fort built between 1709 and 1711. During the War of 1812, these fortifications became part of a sprawling British fort comprising almost 40 buildings. Though this defensive post saw no direct action, over 6,000 soldiers were stationed here throughout the war. By 1869, the structures at Fort Chambly had been abandoned and had either fallen apart or been dismantled. Interest in preserving the fort rose in 1881 when a monument to Charles de Salaberry was unveiled in Chamby. Local citizen Joseph-Octave Dion was given full charge of the restoration of the fort through financial support provided by the Department of Public Works. Fort Chambly was designated a National Historic Site in 1920 and a National Historic Park in 1921. The site is open to the public from May to October.

The guardhouse that resides on the edge of the park is the only remaining building that was part of the British military camp during the War of 1812. Some of the activities and exhibits in the interpretation centre and museum are focused on the history of New France, but much can be gleaned about the fort's role during the War of 1812. In addition to learning about the evolution of the fort, you will explore aspects of garrison life, clothing, and artillery. Exhibits also discuss past archaeological digs of the site and the numerous items and structures which have been found during excavations of the site. For more information visit pc.gc.ca/lhn-nhs/qc/fortchambly/index.aspx

A colourized version of William Henry Bartlett's 1840 painting *Fort Chambly.*

Tour

End your tour of Chambly at the bronze memorial in honour of Charles de Salaberry. (*GPS – 400 de Salaberry St. Chambly, QC*) The monument was erected on 26 October 1881 and is accessible at the corner of Bourgogne Ave. and Salaberry St. It is one of the most beautiful monuments you will see on any tour.

282   L'OPINION PUBLIQUE   16 JUIN 1881

MONUMENT DE SALABERRY À CHAMBLY

An 1881 publication features the de Salaberry Bronze Statue in Chambly.

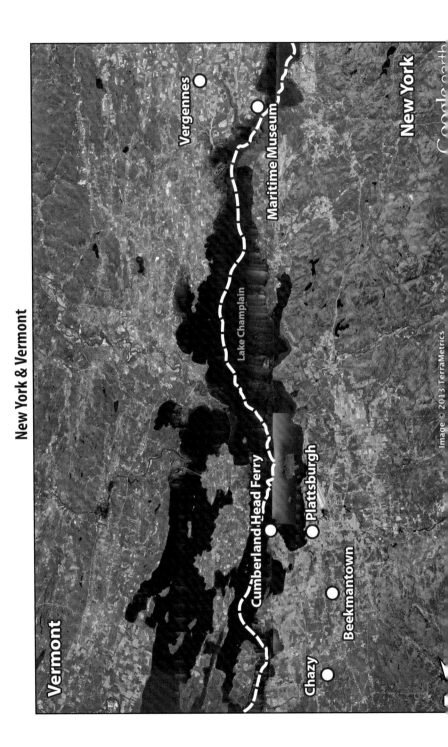

New York & Vermont

Vermont

New York

Vergennes

Maritime Museum

Lake Champlain

Cumberland Head Ferry

Plattsburgh

Beekmantown

Chazy

Image © 2013 TerraMetrics

Crossing the Border: New York & Vermont

The opening stages of the Battle of Plattsburgh, 6-11 September 1814, occurred in the towns of Chazy and Beeksmantown. As the British pushed the Americans southward towards Plattsburgh, homes, churches, and even pubs became collateral damage. Farmlands were converted into camps and houses into headquarters as British and American armies came to a head in multiple skirmishes. If there is one area in the United States that remembers the War of 1812, it is Plattsburgh.

To follow the route the British army took to Plattsburgh, turn off Interstate 87 at Chazy, in Clinton County, New York. There are several buildings and locations worth pointing out along the way. The house which was Sir George Prévost's temporary headquarters on the north side of the Chazy River is intact and marked with a plaque. (*GPS – 9685 New York State Bicycle Rte. 9, Chazy, NY*) Nearby is the small Chazy Public Library which was owned by the law office of Julius C. Hubbell in 1814 and was twice occupied by British forces, first on 9 September during the advance on Plattsburgh and again during their retreat after the battle. (*GPS – 1329 Fiske Rd. Chazy, NY*) At the intersection of Ingraham Rd. and Stratton Hill Rd. sits the Sampsons Tavern where the left wing of General Thomas Brisbane's British army camped on the evening of 5 September 1814. (*GPS – Intersection of Ingraham Rd. and Stratton Hill Rd. Chazy, NY*) Though a historical marker stands on the left side of the driveway, note that this is now a private residence. At the intersection of Spellman Rd. and Rte. 9 is a marker indicating the location of the former Fransworth Tavern. (*GPS – 8033 New York State Bicycle Rte. 9, Plattsburgh, NY*) As the marker describes, according to local tradition the left wing of the British army fired on the tavern on 6 September 1814, thinking it to be a fortification.

Continue down Rte. 22 to follow the series of skirmishes between the Americans and the British right flank from Beekmantown to Plattsburgh. As the British army moved south on 6 September 1814, they encountered a force of 250 Americans at Culver's Hill but were able to repel them. The white farm house just beyond at Rte. 22 and Ashley Rd. is where the fray took place. (*GPS – 6642 New York Rte. 22, Plattsburgh, NY*) During the battle two British leaders, Lieutenant Colonel Wellington and Ensign John Chapman, and one American, Corporal Stephen Partridge, were killed. A monument marking the spot where they fell is located in Culver Hill Historic Park. (*GPS – 571 Spellman Rd. Beekmantown, NY*) Others who died are buried in the earth near where East Beekmantown Cemetery is today. (*GPS – 19 Ashley Rd. Plattsburgh, NY*) A marker by the fence near the road describes the significance of the site.

Tour

Plattsburgh

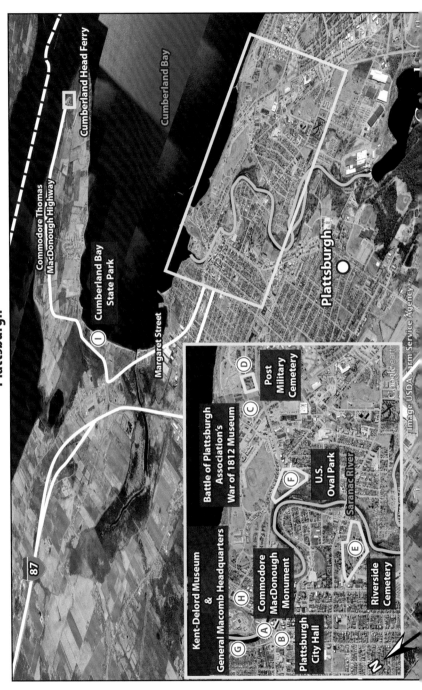

Plattsburgh

(A) Route 22 will take you directly to Plattsburgh. The most striking Plattsburgh monument stands in honour of Commodore Thomas MacDonough, who commanded the American fleet at the battle of Plattsburgh. (*GPS – 42 City Hall Place. Plattsburgh, NY*) You will find this monument in MacDonough Park at the mouth of Cumberland Bay. The 41 metre tall obelisk was dedicated on 18 August 1926 and is made from Indiana limestone topped by a bronze eagle with a seven metre wingspan. The four sides of the monument represent his fleet: *Saratoga*, *Ticonderoga*, *Preble*, and *Eagle*. Interpretative panels bring the past to life on 156 step climb inside the monument. A 360 degree view of the battle grounds awaits those brave enough to take on the climb. The memorial is part of the Plattsburgh National Historic Landmark which is made up of three distinct sites: the MacDonough Monument, Cumberland (Plattsburgh) Bay, and Fort Brown.

The Monument to Commodore MacDonough and City Hall. [Clayton Smalley]

(B) Across from MacDonough Park is Plattsburgh's City Hall which has one of the original anchors from the British flagship *Confiance* on display in the main lobby. (*GPS – 41 City Hall Place. Plattsburgh, NY*) The 3,000 pound, 14-foot anchor was discovered in Cumberland Bay in 1996, raised from the floor in 1998, and put on display in 2000. You can still see a massive cannonball dent in one of the anchor's flukes, as well as the date and place it was manufactured (1813, Quebec).

Tour

(C) The Battle of Plattsburgh Association War of 1812 Museum, open from Wednesday to Saturday, is very highly recommended. (*GPS – 31 Washington Rd. Plattsburgh, NY*) Displays of original works of art related to the war and special exhibits are on view in the KeyBank Gallery. The Allan S. Everett interpretive center, which is part of the museum, features a large interactive timeline of the battle and a detailed diorama of the village as it was in 1814. There are also scale models of the ships engaged in the battle.

(D) Behind the museum, at the intersection of U.S. Ave and Lake Forest Drive, sits the Post Military Cemetery. (*GPS – 4989 U.S. Ave. Plattsburgh, NY*) It is located on the grounds of the former air force base at Plattsburgh, referred to locally as the "Old Base." The site contains a monument to Unknown Dead of the War of 1812. 136 unknown soldiers are buried here in addition to a number of

Watch for these blue and yellow sign posts in Plattsburgh.

soldiers' graves from the War of 1812. The remains of many of these soldiers were discovered while excavating in and around Plattsburgh Barracks.

(E) The Riverside Cemetery also contains burials of British and American soldiers killed during the War of 1812. (*GPS – Riverside Cemetery on Steltzer Rd. Plattsburgh, NY*) If you walk through the graveyard searching for some of these gravestones, look for "Mooers," "Norcross," "Powers," "Wright," all soldiers killed at Plattsburgh. Look also for Joseph Baron, pilot of the *Confiance*, and Captain George Downie of the Royal Navy.

(F) U.S. Oval Park was the site of at least three fortifications occupied during the battle of Plattsburgh and today it is surrounded by ruins and markers indicating their locations. Fort Brown served as the left flank of defence during the Battle of Plattsburgh and is the only fort in Plattsburgh which has any surviving ruins on the surface. (*GPS – 5220 Peru St. Plattsburgh, NY*) A small monument marks the spot where the fort stood and a five-sided outline of a grassy earthworks, ditches, and the remains of some gun placements are all that remains of the site. Fort Moreau was the centre and key point of the American line during the battle. (*GPS – 100 U.S. Oval. Plattsburgh, NY*) Last, Fort Scott stood on the right flank of the American defence. (*GPS – 68 U.S. Oval. Plattsburgh, NY*) Plaques are placed at all of these sites and visiting them is a worthwhile exercise in visualizing the American defence system. Be sure to also stop at the nearby the replica blockhouse. (*GPS – 43 Hamilton St. Plattsburgh, NY*)

G Within the city centre are a number of houses that were occupied by the British or American army during the Battle of Plattsburgh and have survived into the 21st century. The most popular is the Kent-Delord Museum. The residence of the Kent-Delord Museum was occupied by a group of junior artillery officers in September 1814. (*GPS – 17 Cumberland Ave. Plattsburgh, NY*) The house was chosen for its strategic location at the mouth of the Sarnac River and Lake Champlain and received minimal damage during the fighting. A centrepiece of the museum's collection is a tea chest and belongings left behind by a British soldier.

H Of the many others historic buildings to visit the house of Major General Benjamin Mooers is a local legend. The house served as the headquarters for General Alexander Macomb during the battle. (*GPS – 106 Bridge St. Plattsburgh, NY*) The residence is known for the cannonball that entered through an open door and lodged itself in the south wall of the house, where is remains today. A plaque was erected in 1895 by the Saranac Chapter of the Daughters of the American Revolution.

I Cumberland Bay State Park is a popular tourist area that has two spots related to the war which can be viewed during a short walk in the park. (*GPS – 152 Cumberland Head Rd. Plattsburgh, NY*) Near the entrance of the Park is a tombstone monument to 13 unknown soldiers who died of cholera in 1812 and were buried in the vicinity. Secondly, between Cumberland Rd. and Beach Rd. are five consecutive Heritage Trail Markers describing the Battle of Plattsburgh.

The national landmark that overlooks the bay. [Matt Ryan]

Tour

Vergennes

A The ferry from Cumberland Head to Vermont takes you south to Vergennes. Here MacDonough built much of his fleet in 1814. The ferry ride (just 12 minutes) and the drive through beautiful Vermont scenery is most enjoyable. An attractive monument to MacDonough sits in a public park in the city centre and describes the role of shipbuilding in Vergennes and MacDonough's role in the Battle of Plattsburgh. (*GPS – 6 N Green St. Vergennes, VT*) The 3.6 metre high memorial was dedicated in 1925.

A 1913 photo of the monument honouring MacDonough in Vergennes.

B For those fascinated with the history of comemoration, there is a 1914 stone monument in honour of Commodore MacDonough erected by the Daughters of the American Revolution. (*GPS – 36 MacDonough Dr. Vergennes, VT*)

C Cross the river and turn right at the sign for Falls Parks. The original shipyard was located the base of the falls and the park and is well marked. (*GPS – 60 Mechanic St. Vergennes, VT*)

D Here you can also visit the Lake Champlain Maritime Museum, which has an active Marine Archaeology program and an extensive collection of well preserved boats from various eras of Lake Champlain's history. (*GPS – 4472 Basin Harbor Rd. Vergennes, VT*) The museum offers a lake cruise and admission for $28.00. See the range of 1812 activites offered by the museum at lcmm.org.

A view from the top of Otter Creek Falls. Across the river sits the former grounds of Commodore MacDonough's Naval Shipyard. [Jay Parker]

Tour

Touring the Maritimes

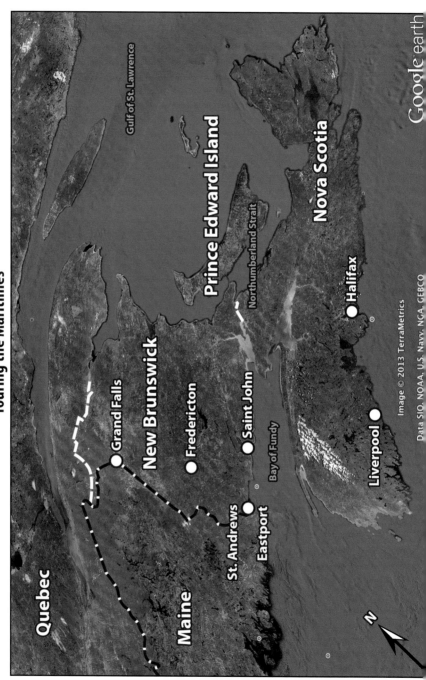

Quebec

Maine

New Brunswick

Grand Falls

Fredericton

Saint John

St. Andrews

Eastport

Bay of Fundy

Gulf of St. Lawrence

Prince Edward Island

Northumberland Strait

Nova Scotia

Halifax

Liverpool

N

Google earth

Image © 2013 TerraMetrics

Data SIO, NOAA, U.S. Navy, NGA, GEBCO

Touring the Maritimes

If you have never visited the East Coast of Canada, hopefully this guide gives you an excuse to visit one of the most beautiful regions in the country. With the exception of Saint John and Halifax, the Atlantic Provinces missed much of the mass industrialization of the late 19th century. The result is two provinces that radiate a natural beauty that is complemented by the friendly and slower pace of life.

In New Brunswick, the Bay of Fundy was considered internationally for the "new seven wonders of the world." The highest tides in the world shape a coastal landscape that is as picturesque as it is adventurist. The trails and waterways that exist within the borders of Fundy National Park are hard to do justice too. The rivers that run through the middle of the province offer some of the world's finest salmon fishing. To plan your trip through New Brunswick visit tourismnewbrunswick.ca

Nova Scotia is another picturesque province that has some of the oldest historical connections to the foundation of Canada. Cape Breton is a 3-hour drive from the provincial border but the Cabot Trail is nothing shy of an outdoorsmen's paradise. The historical enthusiast will not want to leave the province without experiencing the preserved history at the Louisbourg National historic site. Visit novascotia.com to learn more about what the province has to offer.

The tours take you through the key remaining sites during the War of 1812 in the Maritimes. It is worth taking the time to truly experience what the region has to offer outside of the suggestions of this guide.

The autumn harvest in Penniac, New Brunswick. [Martin Cathrae]

New Brunswick

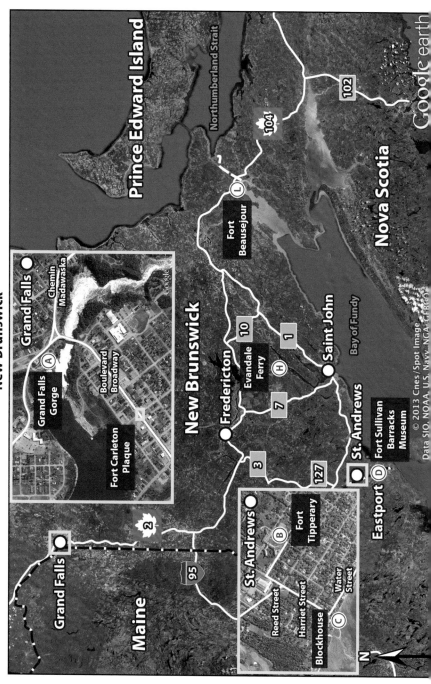

The War of 1812 in New Brunswick was relatively quiet compared to the Upper and Lower Canadian theatres. New Brunswick's role was primarily maritime and economic. New Brunswicker's fought at sea from the outset in the small ship privateering war. During the winter when the St. Lawrence River was impassable, the St. John River system was the only line of communications between the Canadas and Great Britain. At the request of the colony, Eastern Maine was invaded and annexed in 1814. Most important, the freeports of Saint John, St. George, and St. Andrews played key roles in disrupting American trade and in the financial ruin that led to the end of the war. The Treaty of Ghent, reestablished the old New Brunswick/Maine border.

As you enter Northern New Brunswick, thick forests line the highway. It is immediately obvious why the timber resources of the province were valued by the Royal Navy. The woodlands, in a much different capacity, continue to dominate the regional economy. You are also following, in reverse, the long march of the 104th (New Brunswick) Regiment of Foot.

(A) Stopping in Grand Falls breaks up the drive nicely. Here there is a plaque commemorating Fort Carleton on Broadway Blvd. The real highlight though, is the gorge (*GPS – 25 Madawaska Rd. Grand Falls, NB*) that captivated Lieutenant John Le Couteur of the 104th Regiment of Foot:

After dinner most of the officers went to see the fall, it presented a magnificent and curious spectacle. In summer it is 84 feet high and 900 feet in width but it was now greatly reduced, by the quantity of ice which environed it. The spray having frozen as it rose had gradually condensed

The gorge in Grand Falls. [Tourism NB]

itself that it had joined and formed a splendid, irregular, fantastic arch, of surprising brilliancy and lightness, in all the rugged and mixed varieties of form, which frost gives to falling water, suddenly arrested by congelation...The scene called to mind the idea of an enchanted palace of glass, fitter for men to gaze on than inhabit, which was strictly true for desolation reigned around; no beast, bird or even insect cheered the sight or enlivened the ear, the only sound that disturbed the icy deathlike stillness around was the relentless roaring river, rushing impatiently through its restricted and fringed bed of ice...

Next stop in the lovely seaside resort town of St. Andrews. The close proximity to the United States border made St. Andrews both vulnerable to attack and important as a port of entry for food and other supplies via licensed trade or more illicit means from the New England States. The sites of St. Andrews can make for a lovely walk in the small waterfront village.

B The central defensive point of St. Andrews was Fort Tipperary. (*GPS – 69 Prince of Wales St. Andrews, NB*) Fort Tipperary was built in 1808 during the threat of war between Great Britain and the United States over the *Chesapeake* Affair. It was a star-shaped defensive work located on a strategic hill, which commanded the town of St. Andrews, the harbour, and part of the adjacent country. The earthen ramparts still exist at the corner of Prince of Wales and Elisabeth St. next to the famous Algonquin Hotel. Please note that they are now on private property, however they are close by the road and easily visible.

The West Blockhouse in St. Andrews. [Jeffrey W. Mott]

C Led by Robert Pagan and Christopher Scott, who were unwilling to wait for government funding, the private citizens of St. Andrews built three blockhouses to protect the harbour and town. They built one at each entrance of the harbour. A third blockhouse was built upriver from the harbour at Joe's Point. The site of the Joe's Point Blockhouse is now the tee box of the spectacular 12th Hole of the Algonquin Golf Course. The west blockhouse and battery still stands and is a National Historic site. (*GPS – 1 Joes Point Rd. St. Andrews, NB*). The Niger Reef Tea House overlooks the blockhouse and is an excellent spot for refreshment after touring the town and sites.

St. Andrews is famous for whale watching. Other tour operators based in the area also give visitors the chance to see the Passamaquoddy Bay area from the water. On the water it is easy to see why smuggling thrived in the area with the many islands and coves that offered protection. This protection was multiplied by foggy weather which made detection more difficult and navigation treacherous.

The Cannons in St. Andrews. [Jeffrey W. Mott]

D Eastport, Maine, which lies little over an hour's drive from St. Andrews, is well worth a visit. Eastport or Moose Island as the British called it was a disputed island and important smuggling entrepôt, until it was captured in 1814 by the British. If you are there between July and August visit the Fort Sullivan Barracks Museum. (*GPS – 74 Washington St. Eastport, Maine*)

From St. Andrews continue to Saint John via the gorgeous coastal routes. St. George and Dipper Harbour (Rte. 790) were important ports of refuge and were protected with fortifications at the time. Unfortunately none of those fortifications have survived. Visitors do get a sense of the beautiful yet treacherous coast that claimed many mariners during the war, including most of the crew of the HMS *Plumper* which struck a ledge and sank off Dipper Harbour during a snow squall 5 December 1812.

Saint John was the principal port of the province and was protected by several fortifications and batteries. The geography of the area forced a complex and dispersed set of fortifications and requires a car to visit.

Tour

Saint John

(E) It is best to start at the most enduring of 1812 sites in Saint John, the
Carleton Martello Tower. (*GPS – 454 Whipple St. Saint John, NB*) The
stonework tower was actually not completed until after the war. It is an
excellent example of the Martello tower type fortifications built by the
British, inspired by the obstinate defence by a fortified lighthouse in Cape
Mortolla in Corsica in 1794. The tower remained an important part of Saint
John's defences, acting as the fire control centre for the cities batteries during
the Second World War. A 1940s addition sits on top of the tower however the
interior has been restored to as it would have been during the War of 1812.
The site offers an excellent view of the harbour and surrounding area. It is
easy to understand when you stand at the site as to why it was chosen to be

Martello Tower in Saint John. [Jeffrey W. Mott]

fortified. There is an excellent museum on site which in addition to the history of the site gives an excellent orientation to the other supporting fortifications.

(F) The original fortification, Fort Frederick, built on the site of a former French fort, Fort Menagoueche was situated at the western end of Harbour Bridge. It suffered from the high tides of the Bay of Fundy and was dominated by the Carleton Heights a kilometre to the west of the position. Nothing remains at the site. Fort Frederick was proved ineffective during American raids during the American Revolution. In order to deny entrance to the St. John River system and protect the line of communications with the Upper and Lower Canada, Fort Howe was constructed on the limestone hills north of the harbour. The Fort Howe site is marked by a Historical Site Plaque and has a reproduction blockhouse on the site. (*GPS – Magazine St. Saint John, NB*)

(G) Be sure to visit the New Brunswick Museum (nbm-mnb.ca). (*GPS – 1 Market Sq. Saint John, NB*) Among the many artefacts in the museums collections relating to the 1812 era the most spectacular are the regimental colours of the 104th Regiment of Foot (New Brunswick). Raised as the New Brunswick Regiment of Fencible Infantry in 1803 the regiment was elevated to line status in 1810. The regiment began the war garrisoning the province but was ordered to march to Kingston in the winter of 1813. Six companies completed the 1,100km march; the slowest accomplished the feat in 57 days. The regimental colours were nearly consumed in a fire along the way when a temporary hut made of spruce bows caught fire. The regiment served on the Niagara frontier and at Fort Wellington, and was awarded the battle honour NIAGARA.

Fort Howe in Saint John. [Greg Hickman]

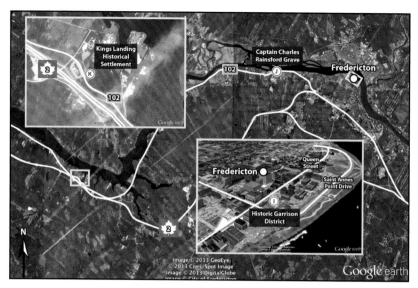

Fredericton

(**H**) From Saint John continue to Fredericton via Rte 7 or the longer but more scenic Rte 102 which follows the river, the route used in the 1812 era. During the War of 1812 the province maintained an armed flotilla to protect the river. A fortified post was maintained at Tenants Cove near the Evandale Ferry (*GPS – Evandale, NB*) on an outcropping known by the French as the *nid d'aigle* or Eagles Nest.

(**I**) The sites in Fredericton make for a nice walk around the Historic Garrison District of the provincial capital. Begin with the Fredericton Region Museum located in the Officers' Quarters in Officers Square. (*GPS – 571 Queen St. Fredericton, NB*) They have many artefacts relating to the War of 1812 including a New Brunswick Regiment of Fencible Infantry uniform. During the summer visitors can watch the changing of the guard in the square and a demonstration of 1812 drill. There is a plaque commemorating the March of the 104th at the Soldiers Barracks on Queen St. If you stop for lunch, try the local favourite Garrison District Ale House on Queen St. Visit yorksunburymuseum.com for more information

(**J**) The final resting place of Captain Charles Rainsford of the 104th Regiment sits at the St. Peter's Anglican Church cemetery. (*GPS – 2365 Woodstock Rd. Fredericton, NB*) Captain Rainsford participated in the epic winter march of the 104th and led a rescue mission when two companies became storm stayed at Lac Temiscouata in Québec. With two companions Rainsford snowshoed in the midst of a blizzard over 145km in two days to locate food and return to the starving soldiers. After the war he was awarded with a pension and a grant of land for his heroism.

The grave of Captain Charles Rainsford. [J. Brent Wilson]

(K) Not far from Fredericton sits the Kings Landing Historical Settlement. (*GPS – 5804 Rte. 102. Prince William, NB*) Kings Landing is a living museum that brings life in the 1800s alive. Churning butter, splitting logs, spinning wool, forging nails, and watching the animals at work – especially on the horse-powered dog saw – are all part of the activities you can engage with. The living museum is designed for a full day of family fun. You can also find the house of Daniel Morehouse a Loyalist settler who lodged officers of the 104th Regiment during their epic winter march to Kingston. See kingslanding.nb.ca for more information

(L) If you are continuing from Fredericton to the Nova Scotia tour of 1812, don't miss Fort Beausejour / Fort Cumberland. (*GPS – 111 Fort Beausejour Rd. Aulac, NB*) (pc.gc.ca/lhn-nhs/nb/beausejour/index.aspx) Located on the Chignecto Isthmus connecting New Brunswick with Nova Scotia. The site has a rich historical significance dating from its construction as a French Fort prior to the Seven Years War. During the War of 1812 its strategic importance had waned, however it remained garrisoned for the duration of the war, safeguarding land communications between New Brunswick and Nova Scotia.

Tour

Nova Scotia

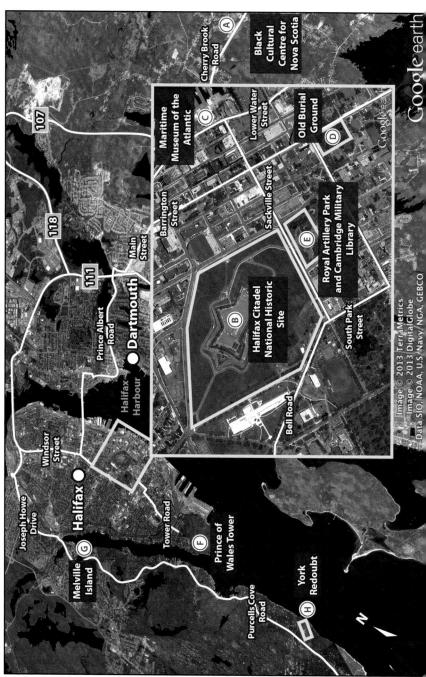

Nova Scotia

Halifax was arguably the most important naval base for the British during the War of 1812. As the primary British base for the Royal Navy's North Atlantic squadron, Halifax served a critical defensive and strategic purpose during the war. The Royal Navy's blockade of the American coast during the War of 1812 crippled the American economy and put immense pressure on the American ability to wage war. The pivotal location of the naval yard allowed for repairs and refits to be done closer to the action. Halifax was the staging point for the expeditions against Maine and the Chesapeake Bay. The port city was well protected by a series of fortifications from the mouth of the Halifax harbour inland. Though never attacked during the War of 1812, the importance of Halifax was clear and in the years following the conflict with America, the Halifax Citadel was completely rebuilt into one of the most powerful fortifications on the Continent. The harbour retains its importance in the modern era as the home of the Royal Canadian Navy Atlantic Fleet.

A In order to undermine the American economy, especially in the Southern States, the Royal Navy actively encouraged slaves to escape to ships operating along the coast. Many of the escaped slaves settled in Nova Scotia. If you are travelling from New Brunswick, stop first at the Black Cultural Centre for Nova Scotia covers the history of the African refugees, including their activities during the War of 1812. (*GPS – 10 Cherry Brook Rd. Cherry Brook, NS*) For more information see bccns.com.

B Stop next at the Halifax Citadel. (*GPS – 5425 Sackville St. Halifax, NS*) The Citadel has a long and rich history that dates back to 1749 and the founding of Halifax. Built on the high ground overlooking the harbour, the fortification that sits on the hill today has been restored to their 1850s

The Halifax Citadel as it stands today. [Nova Scotia Tourism]

Tour

configuration. Every day at noon, the gun blast signals mid-day. There are excellent exhibits on the history of the fortifications and an Army Museum. Guided tours are available as well various programs for all ages, including a ghost tour for those looking for a unique experience. To learn more about the living history at the Halifax Citadel visit pc.gc.ca/lhn-nhs/ns/halifax/visit.aspx.

An 1890s postcard of the view from the Halifax Citadel. [Government of Nova Scotia]

(C) If the weather in Halifax, forces you indoors visit the The Maritime Museum of the Atlantic covers the rich maritime history of the city and region including the War of 1812 era. (*GPS – 1675 Lower Water St. Halifax, NS*) It covers far more than the war but is well worth a stop if you have time. For more information see museum.gov.ns.ca/mmanew/en/home/default.aspx. If you can, visit Halifax during the annual Tall Ships Festival when once again square rigged sailing vessels populate the harbour.

(D) It was in Halifax where the USS *Chesapeake* was brought after its capture by the HMS *Shannon*. Captain James Lawrence of the USN *Chesapeake* was initially buried in the "Old Burial Ground." (*GPS – 1460 Barrington St. Halifax, NS*) Later his body was exhumed and re-interred in Trinity Church Cemetary in New York City. The Old Burial Ground, also known as St. Paul's Church Cemetery remains the final resting place of Major General Robert Ross who led the ground forces that captured Washington, DC. Ross, who died in battle outside of Baltimore was later transported to Halifax. Also laid to rest here is Sergeant Richard Smith of the 104th Regiment. Sergeant Smith was in the Grenadier Company of the 104th and was apart of the "forlorn hope" or the lead assault element during the assault on Fort Erie 15 August 1814 where he was wounded and lost an arm. He survived and later served as a magistrate before his death at age 28.

The grave of Sergeant Smith. [Jeffrey W. Mott]

(**E**) You might decide to visit the Cambridge Military Library. (*GPS – 1575 Queen St. Halifax, NS*) The library was built with resources from the Castine Fund, the tariffs collected by the British in their short lived occupation of Castine, Maine at the mouth of the Penobscot River. You must call ahead to arrange a tour (902-427-4494). The remainder of the Castine fund went to the formation of Dalhousie College, now Dalhousie University.

(**F**) Next visit the Halifax fortification, the Prince of Wales Tower, at the tip of the harbour in Point Pleasant Park. (*GPS – 508 Tower Rd. Halifax, NS*) The National Historic Site was initially designed to protect the city and provide early warning of an attack. Fitted with six mounted guns on the roof and four more on the second story, the tower was an imposing

An 1890s photograph of the Prince of Wales Tower. [Government of Nova Scotia]

defensive fortification in the early 19th century. The fort continued to be a strategic observation post until the end of the Second World War. The original tower still stands and the large seaside tract of land is now a beautiful park and the perfect place for a picnic or an afternoon hike.

(G) The war left its mark in Halifax in other ways as well. Prisoners of war were held on Melville Island, now the location of the Armdale Yacht Club. (*GPS – 75 Burgee Run, Halifax*) Many POWs did not survive; 188 American POWs are buried at nearby Dead Man's Island Park. (*GPS – 24 Pine Haven Dr. Halifax, NS*) A commemorative plaque has been placed there in their memory, listing the names and ships they served on.

(H) If you are keen on visiting the other fortifications of the city you will want to see the York Redoubt. (*GPS – York Redoubt Cres. Halifax, NS*) Originally built in 1798, the fortification became an essential link in the communication in and around the harbour. It was reconstructed and refitted many times during the 19th and 20th centuries. The site today is mostly closed to the public but the drive along the coast is lovely and once you are at the site its geographic importance is clear.

An 1817 sketch of the York Redoubt with the Martello Tower in the distance. [Government of Nova Scotia]

The maritime conflict was not limited to the ships of the Royal Navy. One of the major centres of privateering activity was in Liverpool. (*GPS – 109 Main St. Liverpool, NS*) The stunning hour and half drive along the coast from Halifax will take you to this small cove. The most famous privateering vessel was the *Liverpool Packet*, which captured over 50 vessels during its career. The *Liverpool Packet* was owned by Enos Collins who later formed the Halifax Banking Company a forerunner of the Canadian Imperial Bank of Commerce (CIBC). In Liverpool be sure to visit the Queens County Museum (queenscountymuseum.com).

Tour

Further Reading

The biographies of the British, Canadian, and First Nations participants in the War of 1812, published by the Dictionary of Canadian Biography are available on the web at DCB online, provide fascinating background and should be your first choice. John Sugden's biography, *Tecumseh* (1998), is the best available book-length study of this enigmatic warrior. You may also enjoy Wesley B. Turner, *The Astonishing General: The Life and Legacy of Isaac Brock* (2011). Sandy Amtal, A Wampum Denied, *Proctor's Way of 1812* (2011) raises new questions about Tecumseh and Brock and tries to rehabilitate Proctor.

Books on specific battles or campaigns that offer tactical, "sharp end" accounts include Donald E. Graves *Red Coats and Grey Jackets: The Battle of Chippawa* (1994), *Field of Glory: The Battle of Crysler's Farm 1813* (1999) and *Where Right and Glory Lead!: The Battle of Lundy's Lane* (1997). Robert Malcomson *Capital in Flames: The American Attack on York* (2008) James Elliott Strange *Fatality: The Battle of Stoney Creek* (2009) Allan Everest *The War of 1812 in the Champlain Valley* (1981) Joseph Whitehorne *While Washington Burned: The Battle of Fort Erie* (2006) Robin Reilly's *The British at the Gates: the New Orleans Campaign in the War of 1812* (2002). Robert L. Dallison, *A Neighbourly War: New Brunswick and the War of 1812* (2012) captures the conflict in the Maritimes. Barry Gough *Through Water, Ice, and Fire: The Schooner 'Nancy' of the War of 1812* (2006). JCA Stagg, the author of *Mr. Madison's War* the exhaustive study of American policy has a new overview of the events, *The War of 1812: Conflict for a Continent* (2012). Alan Taylor's book, *The Civil War of 1812* (2010) and George Daughan *1812: The Navy's War* (2012) have attracted favourable reviews.

Donald Hickey's books include *Don't Give Up the Ship: Myths of the War of 1812* (2006) and the well-illustrated *The Rocket's Red Glare* (2011). George Stanley's *The War of 1812* (1983) should be available at your local library.

Websites to Consult

There are hundreds of websites offering information about major battles, prominent individuals, and historic sites associated with the War of 1812. We especially recommend using the Dictionary of Canadian Biography online (search "DCB online"). These well-researched biographies of British, Canadian, and First Nations participants are highly recommended. Unfortunately the Dictionary of American Biography requires a membership fee. *The Pictorial Field-Book of the War of 1812* by Benson J. Lossing originally published in 1869 is freely available through ancestry.com (It is the first Google hit for the search term Lossings 1812) and provides an excellent visual reference for the era. Wherever you see [Lossing] you will find those images in his original text as well. There are several sites listed within the touring section that should help you navigate unfamiliar territory. Be sure to consult northamericanforts.com which is particularly useful as it provides links to the most valuable websites. The Niagara Parks Commission also has a very helpful website on the many War of 1812 sites (niagaraparks.com/heritage-trail). Exploring the web will provide information on activities planned for 2013 and 2014 in your area.

Our site, canadianmilitaryhistory.ca, is geared toward research, education and discussion of historical and contemporary conflict. We encourage you to take in our weekly updates and engage in the discussion.

History Section Index

Additional Information

Additional Information

Tour Section Index

Additional Information

Gage Homestead 193-194
Grand Falls, New Brunswick 241
Green, Billy 195
Gunboat (Fort Wellington) 159

Halifax, Nova Scotia 249-252
Hamilton, Ontario 191-192
Hamilton and Scourge Navy Memorial
Garden 195-196
Hancock and Dean Bridge 139-140
Harrison, William 129, 141
Historic Sites and Monuments Board 121-122

Joe's Point Blockhouse 243

Kent Volunteers 127
Kentucky Militia 149, 153
Key, Francis Scott 120
Kings Landing 247
Kingston 155, 163-165

Lacolle Blockhouse 223, 225
Lacolle, Battles of 223, 225
Laura Secord Homestead 203-204
Lake Champlain Maritime Museum 237
Lake Erie, Battle of 134-135, 214
Liverpool Packet, schooner 252
Longwoods, Battle of 127-128
Lundy's Lane, Battle of 209

MacDonough, Thomas 233, 237
Macdonell, Lieutenant-Colonel
"Red George" 160
McGregor, John 131
Mackinac Island 180-181
Manitoulin Island 175
Maritime Museum of the Atlantic 250
Martello Towers 163, 165, 244
McFarland House 203
Mohawks 225
Moravians 129
Moraviantown, Battle of 130
Morrisburg, Ontario 157

Morristown, New York 161
Murney Tower 165
Murray's Raid 225

Navy Yard (Amherstburg) 134-135
Navy Yard (Kingston) 163
Niagara Falls Historical Museum 209
Niagara Historical Society and Museum 201
Niagara-on-the-Lake 199-201

Ogdensburg, New York 158-160
Ontario Heritage Foundation 122
Oswego, New York 163

Parks Canada 130
Perry, Oliver Hazard 151
Perrysburg, Ohio 151-152
Pike, Zeublon 171, 185
Plattsburgh, Battle of 231-235
Prescott, Ontario 158-160
Presque Ile State Park (Erie, Pennsylvania) 214-
215
Prince of Wales Tower 251
Put-in-Bay 214-215

Queenston Heights, Battle of 121, 203-207

Rainsford, Captain Charles 246
Riall, Phineas 210
River Canard 139-140
River Raisin National Battlefield Park 147-149
River Raisin, Battle of 147
Ross, Robert 250
Royal George, HMS 163
Royal Military College 163
Royal Newfoundland Regiment (Fencibles) 189

Sackets Harbor, battlefield 167-171
Saint John, New Brunswick 121, 241-245
Sandwich, Ontario 140-142
Sault Ste. Marie 179
Secord, Laura 203, 207, 209-210
Shannon, HMS 250

Additional Information

Contributors

Terry Copp is Professor Emeritus of History at Wilfrid Laurier University and Director of the Laurier Centre for Military Strategic and Disarmament Studies. Copp is an influential advocate for military history in both military and civilian post-secondary education. His volumes, *Battle Exhaustion* (1990), *The Brigade* (1992), *Fields of Fire* (2003) and *Cinderella Army* (2006), have led to a reinterpretation of Canadians in the Second World War. Copp's interest in the battlefields of Europe led to the creation of memorials and study tours for teacher and students, and the publication of invaluable battlefield guides to Canadian participation in both world wars. He is also the founder of *Canadian Military History*, Canada's leading journal of military history. Copp conceived of the project, wrote the history section and sketched out the tour sections of the guide.

Matt Symes is the Publications Manager for LCMSDS, the editor of canadianmilitaryhistory.ca and a PhD Candidate (ABD) at Wilfrid Laurier University. *1812: A Guide to the War and its Legacy* is the fifth battlefield guide that Symes has worked on. He was responsible for writing parts of the tour section, the final edits, as well as the design and layout of the guide.

Caitlin McWilliams is an MA (History) graduate from Wilfrid Laurier University and a Research Associate at LCMSDS. Drawing on her educational and battlefield touring experience as well as her photography talent, McWilliams scouted, wrote, edited and/or added photographs to parts of every tour section in the guide.

Nick Lachance is a student at Wilfrid Laurier University and a Research Assistant at LCMSDS. Many of his photos appear in this guide. Lachance's primary responsibility was to use modern satellite images from Google Earth and rework them into the 59 historical and tour maps inside the guide.

Geoff Keelan is a PhD Candidate (ABD) at the University of Waterloo and a Research Associate at LCMSDS. As a veteran of many European battlefield tours, he and Nick Lachance travelled to many of the locations in the tour section. He used that experience to write several of the tour sections.

Jeffrey W. Mott is an MA (History) graduate from the University of New Brunswick. He has worked extensively on the War of 1812 for the Gregg Centre at UNB and for the St. John River Society. Mott was responsible for adding the historical context of the war in what is now New Brunswick and Nova Scotia, in addition to writing the touring sections for the two provinces.

Additional Information

264